Understanding Learners in Open and Distance Education

WITHDRAWN

Open and Distance Learning Series

Series Editor: Fred Lockwood

OPEN AND DISTANCE LEARNING SERIES

Understanding Learners in Open and Distance Education

TERRY EVANS

KOGAN PAGE
Published in association with the
Institute of Educational Technology, Open University

First published in 1994

Kogan Page Limited
120 Pentonville Road
London N1 9JN

© Terry Evans, 1994

British Library Cataloguing in Publication Data

A CIP record for this book is available from the British Library.

ISBN 0 7494 1235 6

Typeset by BookEns Ltd, Baldock, Herts.
Printed and bound in Great Britain by
Biddles Ltd, Guildford and King's Lynn

Contents

Acknowledgements

I would like to thank Helen Carley, Lesley Evans, Philip Juler, Fred Lockwood and Daryl Nation for their advice, encouragement and criticism in the writing of this book.

Series editor's foreword

The use of open and distance learning is increasing dramatically in all sections of education and training. This increase is occurring both in the UK and around the world. Many schools, colleges, universities, companies and organizations are already using open and distance learning practices in their teaching and training and want to develop these further. Furthermore, many individuals have heard about open and distance learning and would welcome the opportunity to find out more about it and explore its potential.

Whatever your current interest in open and distance learning and experience within it, I believe there will be something in this series of short books for you. The series is directed at teachers, trainers, educational advisers, in-house training managers and training consultants involved in designing open and distance learning systems and materials. It will be invaluable for those working in learning environments ranging from industry and commerce to public sector organizations, from schools and colleges to universities.

This series is designed to provide a comprehensive coverage of the field of open and distance learning. Each title focuses on a different aspect of designing and developing open and distance learning and provides concrete advice and information, which is built upon current theory and research in the field and how it relates to actual practice. This basis, of theory, research and development experience, is unique in the area of open and distance learning. I say this with some confidence since the Open University Institute of Educational Technology, from which virtually all the authors are drawn, contains the largest collection of educational technologists (course designers, developers and researchers) in the world. Since the inception of the Open University in 1969, members of the Institute have made a major contribution to the design and production of learning systems and materials not just in the Open University but in many other organizations in this country and elsewhere. We would now like to share our experience and findings with you.

In this book, *Understanding learners in open and distance education*, the unique world of the learner is explored – in the words of the learners themselves. It shatters the comfortable but misguided assumption that we can regard students as a homogeneous group. Terry illustrates, at times subtlely and at others forcibly, how different the students are and how previous experience and present circumstances influence their learning.

The book identifies the main factors likely to influence a learner in their study: money, sex, power, age, work and leisure. While many of us would acknowledge the influence of these I suspect few of us would appreciate how powerful their influences are and the effects on the learner. The insights Terry gives us will make us reconsider how much we think we know about our own learners and how much more we need to know.

A major feature of the book is the relaxed and engaging style it adopts. While other authors have tried to alert us to the importance of understanding the context of a student's study, they have often left the reader swamped in a complex mass of theoretical frameworks, abstract concepts and academic argument. Although this book is based firmly on acknowledged theory and substantial research evidence the simplicity of explanation, and judicious use of end notes, enhances rather than detracts from the case being made.

I am sure you will enjoy this book and it will encourage you to strive for a better understanding of your students – to everyone's benefit.

Fred Lockwood

Chapter 1

Introduction

Understanding learners

Don Markovitz left a chilly December in Manchester to attend a conference in Melbourne on new approaches to workplace education. Don is the staff training and development manager of a packaging company. The company had experienced considerable difficulties during the 1980s when some of their longstanding customers closed their businesses and others reduced their packaging requirements. New European standards for packaging, together with the Green movement's lobbying for 'environmentally friendly' packaging, left the company staring down a slide to insolvency. On a search for new business the sales manager secured a contract with a Scandinavian company to produce a range of packaging for their cosmetics and toiletries. The Scandinavian company not only required types of packaging using recycled plastics which Don's company had not produced before, but also the entire order needed to be 'environmentally friendly' in line with the Scandinavians' corporate image.

Within three years Don's company experienced a substantial shift in its own approaches to business. 'Environmentally friendly' packaging became its profitable core business, and the research and development side of the company expanded to investigate new processes and products to fortify and expand this core. New management practices followed as the 'quality assurance' movement made its mark. Don's position as staff training and development manager was created as a separate area in the Human Resources Division and he experienced a considerable fillip to his job satisfaction and career as the company sought to 'bank their brains'. The training budget had doubled since Don had been manager, largely through his establishment of a range of company-related courses in business, environmental science and technology, and industrial processes, offered to staff through a college and a university department. These courses are taught using both independent study materials and study sessions at the company.

The conference in Melbourne had gone well. His own presentation on his developments in workplace education had been well received and he acquired many ideas and personal contacts. It was his first visit to a large international conference and to have made a successful presentation constituted a significant learning experience for himself. However, he had a little more to learn on this trip yet.

Don caught the afternoon Qantas flight from Melbourne to Manchester. It was a bright sunny day and as he looked through the aircraft window from his Business Class seat he thought how clean, green and fresh the countryside appeared and how he felt similarly refreshed and invigorated. Just before departure a woman occupied the seat next to him. They acknowledged each other with the polite apprehension that strangers often do when they are going to spend the next 22 hours together. Orange juice was distributed by a flight attendant, after which came the safety demonstration. The video screens displayed the instructions for oxygen masks and lifejackets as the flight attendants provided the living display. As Don looked around the cabin he noted the ways the 'learners' reacted to the safety demonstration. Although their safety could well depend on it, many of the 'learners' read books or magazines or peered out of the window. These were the 'cool' customers, who had seen this class many times before. A few watched as if their lives did depend on it!

Don noted that his travelling companion had watched the display with some measured care but, like him, had also been looking at the other passengers' responses. The safety display over, Don sparked a conversation by commenting on the way people reacted differently to the safety demonstration. Liz Curie, his fellow passenger, responded that she is always interested in what other people do, but as she had never travelled Business Class before she thought she had better find out where the lifejackets and other safety features were located, just in case. Don revealed that he had just been to a conference where training videos were one of the topics, so he was looking at it in a different light. Liz said that as a school teacher, she was probably just keeping an eye out on what was happening at the back of the class! She was going on holiday to the UK and had been 'upgraded' to Business Class which she thought was a good omen for her holiday. During the course of the flight to Singapore they swapped stories about their work as educators.

Liz told Don that she starts the next school year as the teacher of a class of 7-year-olds and she is somewhat apprehensive about how they will get on. She knows something of the children from their orientation afternoon, but establishing a rapport with a new class is never easy. They were fairly quiet and well-behaved during the orientation afternoon, but three children were away at the time, and her colleague Dave Stark warned her that one of the absentees was capable of disrupting the entire class if the mood took him. However, 'forewarned and forearmed', she estimated that she would give him the opportunity for a fresh start and then pounce if things looked like becoming difficult. Discussions with other colleagues had also provided her with a host of 'staffroom intelligence' on her future charges.

Before flying on the holiday Liz came into school for a day and looked through her new class's records. There were 32 children: 17 girls and 15 boys. One boy had developed muscular dystrophy and was finding it increasingly difficult to walk. He was likely to be using a wheelchair during the year. Liz considered that the class sharing in the experience of his disability could be a positive encounter for them all. His parents were very understanding and cooperative, and they encouraged him to participate in everything he could at school, so Liz felt that she could provide him with a productive year educationally, physically and socially. Eight children were from single or separated parent families. Four children had learning difficulties and were struggling with their reading and writing. Liz had to try and arrest the relative decline in their performance in relation to their peers, otherwise their learning difficulties would become broader educational problems. Five children were from recent immigrant families and, apart from some instances of two Turkish children experiencing childish racist taunts in the playground last year, all five seemed to be settling down and progressing well at school. It seemed that at least six of the children were very bright and had outstanding performances on several educational tests.

Liz knew several of the parents of her class already, either from previous school activities or through the local netball club for which she played with some of the parents. These sorts of contacts provided her with a good deal of local 'intelligence' about the community. She lived outside the school's catchment area but knew its characteristics well. When she first came to the school four years ago she rented a flat in the area and used to walk to school when the weather permitted. Her house-buying searches during her first year provided her with many estate agents' views of which schools were 'good' and 'bad', which areas were 'worth considering' and which were not. Eventually she bought outside the school's area because she thought it better to have some privacy from work. When she looked at the children's files she could make rough assessments of their parents' incomes, educational and social backgrounds from their addresses and occupations. Dave had also given her other information which extended her knowledge of the children. He had taken them away on a two-day camp which meant that he came to know them outside of school. A few parents helped with the children at the camp which enabled him to know those parents better, and he also gleaned information about other parents and their circumstances.

Don commented that when Liz walks into her class on the first day of the year she will know quite a lot about her children: a lot more than the parents and children could have realized. As they prepared to land at Singapore to refuel, Don reflected that he knew quite a lot about his own 'students', but that he had not really considered this as an important part of his job. He usually focused on what was taught, rather than on to whom it was taught. Basic learner considerations were covered, of course, but he pondered on how many of the employees in his company and their contexts he really knew. He wondered fleetingly if Qantas had a better idea of its ever-changing, cosmopolitan 'learners' than he did of the longstanding employees on the company's occupational health and safety course. He learned something on this flight which was largely absent at the conference with its display stands of computer, video and other 'hi-tech' training aids. He smiled as he imagined a display stand full of learners yelling and screaming in a kaleidoscopic visual frenzy reminiscent of a Ken Russell film scene.

Understanding learners in open and distance education

There is a lot of difference between the safety 'class' on an aircraft and the primary school class; Don's training groups fall somewhere in between. Yet it is important in each set of circumstances to know the learners. An airline's problem is very simple in terms of the knowledge and skills which are to be taught but, of course, the passengers are a highly disparate and heterogeneous population. All sorts of languages, disabilities and ages have to be accommodated.

Contrast Liz's knowledge of her 7-year-olds with the knowledge the teacher or trainer in open and distance learning has of their students. In some cases, they may have a good knowledge, if not of the actual people, certainly of the sorts of people they are going to be teaching. For example, some workplace trainers may well know their next group of production supervisors on a quality assurance course because they have taught them on previous courses. But for the majority of those working in open and distance education, they work on developing courses for months and even years before the learners even know of the course's existence, let alone that they are going to decide to enrol in it! In many ways, the construction of the course actually *constructs* the students too. Whether it is a large open university in a third world nation developing a new course on agricultural science, or a training officer in a small company acquiring and modifying an open learning pack on occupational health and safety, both are constructing an educational opportunity which – perhaps through advertising, counselling and/or company, government or union requirements – leads a group of people to become students for part of their lives. Unlike Liz's children, they are rarely compelled to be in education and certainly are unlikely to be compelled to spend as much time at school as her 7-year-olds. For adults, study may be a significant and important part of their lives, but it rarely moves beyond being one part which they have to balance with other things in their lives.

Liz's children, complex individuals though they may be, are relatively simple beings from the adult educator's perspective. In terms of cognitive processes, existing stocks of knowledge, skills and values, previous experiences, worldly responsibilities, their ages and so forth, adult students are typically much more diverse and complex than their 7-year-old counterparts. Of course, some people working in open and distance education teach 7-year-olds and, although they usually have many of the advantages that Liz possesses in terms of having a more prescribed and less diverse clientele, some confront similar difficulties to their adult education counterparts.[1] However, this book is concerned principally with adults, although some of the points covered may well have relevance for teachers of children.

Liz's encounter with Don is illustrative of the tasks that adult educators have before them, especially those in open and distance education. Liz takes a leap of faith when she enters her class for the first time. However, she has many advantages in terms of her existing knowledge of the children and their contexts, her power and authority and her intense classroom interaction with her children. She is able to adapt and adopt her teaching from the outset to unexpected instances and circumstances as they arise. For open and distance educators, such face-to-face contexts are the exception rather than the everyday experience. For them the leap of faith is a bungee jump into the unknown! Most open and distant student learning occurs independently of the teachers' presence, but dependently on the course materials they have prepared. Open and distance teachers and trainers have to make complex educational decisions, if not exactly in the dark, certainly in the gloom of speculation, interpretation, extrapolation and guesswork! Then, if these decisions are in error in some way, this often cannot be discovered, or can only be discovered when it is too late (at least for the first students) as assignments come in or evaluation sheets are returned. Teachers at a distance cannot see the equivalent of the mystified gazes, blank looks or bored faces of Liz's 7-year-olds. Neither can they take the immediate action which Liz can take to remedy the situation. The people who teach Don's courses do have the opportunity to see the looks of their students, but they also have the problems of teaching and learning at a distance for their independent study materials.

Reading this book

What then does this book cover? It deals with the various aspects of learners' engagements with open and distance education in a broadly biographical order. The book commences with the diversities which the open and distance teacher can expect in their learners' backgrounds, that is from their childhood experiences through to the present. The first thoughts of enrolment, through to the issues involved in students' experiences of open and distance education, are presented sequentially. Aspects of students' study lives and the interrelationships with their broader contexts are revealed. These include issues of money, sex, power, age, work and leisure. After glimpsing the diversity in the learners' stories it is intended that the reader will have their own understanding of learners' stories enhanced and, thereby, any notions of homogeneity in prospective or current student bodies will be set aside.

It can be seen that open and distance educators have distinctive problems in comparison with their classroom counterparts. First, they have to do most of their teaching work well before the actual students are known and second, those eventual students will be more diverse, sophisticated, knowledgeable and experienced than their young counterparts in schools. Fred Lockwood's and Alistair Morgan's previous books in this series relate to aspects of the first of the problems above concerning both teaching strategies and learning approaches.[2] This present book deals principally with the second problem. It provides an insight into the main aspects of students' contexts which are often invisible to open and distance educators. These insights are grounded in the stories of students themselves. The stories are woven into the text of the following chapters and are displayed explicitly in a separate typographic format. The contrasts and contradictions, and the diversities and disagreements are shown through the ways different students, in different contexts and with different backgrounds, see and tell their experiences of learning.

The students' stories have been collected over the years that I have been involved in research and evaluation projects in open and distance education. In the course of these projects I have surveyed thousands of students, using questionnaires and I have interviewed hundreds, mostly in their homes or workplaces, but sometimes by telephone. When Fred Lockwood, the series editor, approached me to write this book I had been planning a book based upon some research I had completed with students at my own university, Deakin University in Australia and at the Open University in the United Kingdom where I had spent three months in 1988.[3] Our discussions and my subsequent thinking led me to plan this book as a stage on which many students' stories could be told, based not only on this research, but also drawing on my other work. This other work has included research and consultancy in various forms of open and distance education settings, including workplace education and training, new technologies and professional development.

I believe that it is particularly appropriate if the students' stories are told, as much as possible, in their own words and so I have taken excerpts from transcripts of interviews with students and woven them into each of the main chapters in the book. In order to preserve confidentiality, students' names have been changed and other specific details have been eliminated or modified where necessary. I have revised the excerpts to make them more readable, otherwise the details are as they were told to me by the students. I hope that, as the reader, you can sense the feelings and the people behind the stories. In my view, sensing the feelings and the people behind open and distance education is one of the most important qualities of being a good open and distance educator or trainer. Listening to students, or reading their stories here, is a useful way of enhancing one's sensitivities in this regard still further. It is important to recognize, however, that the excerpts provided here are only small parts of the transcripts from each student – which are in themselves 'frozen' instances of their views at the particular time – and also that they are just solo voices from 'massed choirs' of learners.

In trying to anticipate the readers of this book, I have worked principally with a practitioner focus, rather than with a researcher or theoretician focus. These are not mutually exclusive categories, and I also expect readers with research or theory interests to find much that harmonizes usefully with such interests. Prospective or present students through open or distance education are also part of the intended readership. I hope they find that this book will help them understand that they are not alone 'out there' and that many of the issues which other students describe are ones that they will confront or may be contending with at present. Such understanding not only helps people cope with issues which surround their learning, but it may also help them develop strategies to manage their circumstances better. Students of the theory and practice of open and distance education should also find the book useful; it is for them, and those with research and theory interests, that I have provided the endnotes with either a further comment or reference which may be useful for enquiring further into the field.

Those readers who are familiar with some of my previous work in open and distance education, particularly my work with my friend and colleague Daryl Nation of Monash University, will know that matters of theory are never far from view.[4] In this book, apart from the aforementioned footnotes, I have left formal theoretical discussions aside until I reach the final chapter where I make some theoretical connections, although these are, again, mostly confined to the endnotes. The use of endnotes with full bibliographic detail has removed the need for a separate list of references at the end of the book and, therefore, an index is also largely redundant.

Ideas behind the book

My ideas as a teacher and writer on matters of open and distance education underpin the way this book unfolds. These ideas are pursued further in Chapter 9; however, it is important that a few brief comments are made here to help orientate the reader.

With regard to distance education, some of these ideas concern understanding the distances between distance educators and their students, not just as static distances which can be measured in kilometres or miles. Rather, they are complex and fluid 'distances' in the teacher-learner relationship. These are not just matters of geography or even time; the social, economic, spiritual, political, experiential and personal dimensions add many interwoven layers to the 'distancing' of the teacher from the student. However, understanding something of these layers does allow for some distances to be bridged by distance educators and trainers, rather than being avoided or ignored, and for others to be recognized as salient, if potentially problematic, features of distance education processes.

With regard to open education, the point is more about taking openness to heart and being open to the diversity which shapes and moulds people's learning. Open education is not about 'flexible delivery' (or whatever other term is in vogue); it is about valuing and enhancing the openness of one's teaching or training systems and processes to the needs, interests and contexts of learners, communities, industries or societies more broadly. Hence, I think the common term 'open *learning*' is inappropriate or misses the point. It is the *teaching* or *training* which needs to be open; whether the learning is open or not seems to me to be largely a matter for the learners. The openness of the teaching or training processes may well encourage the learning to be 'open', but what being 'open' really means in terms of the learners' intellectual processes is another matter entirely. Consequently, in this book I shall use the terms 'open education' or 'open and distance education' and by these terms I mean to include both teaching and training – and learning.[5]

I have used the terms 'student' and 'learner' and their derivations more or less interchangeably throughout this book. In most circumstances, students are those who learn as a result of being enrolled formally in courses, therefore one of their roles is as students. Learners are perhaps best seen as people who are engaged in learning as part of another of their roles in life, such as being company staff engaged in a training workshop. So, on these assumptions, all students are learners, but not all learners are students! However, for the purposes of this book the focus is on adults learning and studying through open and distance education.

As each chapter presents the students' stories in relation to the particular issues from their learning contexts, I have included points, arguments or questions which appear pertinent for educators or students in open or distance education. However, in recognizing the diversity of students' contexts one should also recognize that educators' contexts are likewise diverse and so the reader may well find different points, arguments or questions which they would raise for their own contexts. As the author, I hope this reader-inspired reflection occurs. It accords with the sort of approach any practitioner should take to reflecting on their practice.[6] Of course, after the questioning and reflection comes the action! My aim is to provide a book which will lead to action on the part of practitioners to the extent that, by understanding students' contexts better, they are able to improve the open and distance education they provide for their learners.

Notes

1 I am particularly thinking of those teachers in many countries of the world who work in what are called Correspondence Schools, Schools of the Air, Schools of Distance Education, etc. For some such teachers, understanding their children's special circumstances and contexts can be as enlightening as it is challenging. Some useful and interesting writing on such schools is: Ashton, J (1971) *Out of the Silence*, Adelaide: Investigator Press; Gibb, P (1986) *Classrooms a World Apart: The story of Broken Hill School of the Air*, Melbourne: Spectrum Publications; Dewal, O S (1986) *Open School, India: The preliminary years, 1979–1983*, Geelong: Deakin Open Education Monographs; Haughey, M (1990) 'Distance education in schools', *The Canadian Administrator* 29, 8, 1–9; Motley, C and Starr, B (1990) *Bush Tracks and Radio Waves: A history of Port Augusta School of the Air 1958–1990*, Adelaide: Tread Softly Publishing.

2 Fred Lockwood's book, *Activities in Self-instructional Texts* (1992, London: Kogan Page) is specifically focused on approaches for improving active learning through the medium of print. Alistair Morgan's book, *Improving Your Students' Learning* (1993, London: Kogan Page) takes a broad view of student learning and deals with many aspects complementary to the present book.

3 I am grateful to Deakin University for providing sabbatical leave and some research funds for this project and to the Open University for a Visiting Research Fellowship to conduct the UK research.

4 Some key examples of this work can be found in the following references: Evans, T D (1989) 'Taking place: the social construction of place, time and space and the (re) making of distances in distance education', *Distance Education*, 10, 2, 170–83; Evans, T D and Nation, D E (1989) 'Critical reflections in distance education', in Evans, T D and Nation D E (eds) *Critical Reflections on Distance Education*, London: Falmer Press, pp. 237–52; Evans, T D and Nation, D E (1989) 'Dialogue in practice, research and theory in distance education, *Open Learning*, 4, 2, 37–43; Evans, T D and Nation, D E (1992) 'Theorising open and distance education', *Open Learning*, 7, 2, 3–13 (republished in Tait, A (ed.) (1993), *Key Issues in Open Learning*, London: Longman, pp. 45–62); Evans, T D and Nation, D E (1993) 'Education technologies: reforming open and distance education', in Evans, T D and Nation, D E (eds) *Reforming Open and Distance Education: Critical reflections from practice*, London: Kogan Page, pp. 196–214.

5 A debate raged in the journal *Open Learning* in 1989 and 1990 concerning the use of terms such as 'open learning' and 'distance learning'. See, Rumble, G (1989) ' "Open learning", "distance learning", and the misuse of language', *Open Learning*, 4, 2, 28–36 (republished in Tait, A (ed.) (1993) *Key Issues in Open Learning*, London: Longman, pp. 24–44). Derek Rowntree covers the more usual definitions of open learning in a previous book in this series; see, Rowntree, D (1992) *Exploring Open and Distance Learning*, London: Kogan Page.

Ross Paul has written a very stimulating book which considers the broader implications of managing an open education institution; see, Paul, R (1990) *Open Learning and Open Management: Leadership and integrity in distance education*, London: Kogan Page.

6 Donald Schön has provided immense stimulus for thinking of professionals as reflective practitioners; see, for example, Schön, D (1983) *The Reflective Practitioner: How professionals think in action*, New York: Basic Books. In terms of adult learners, others have also dwelt on the significance of the reflection processes in learning and thinking; see, for example, Boud, D, Keogh, R and Walker, D (eds) (1985) *Reflection: Turning experience into learning*, London: Kogan Page; Brookfield, S (1987) *Developing Critical Thinkers: Challenging adults to explore alternative ways of thinking and acting*, San Francisco: Jossey Bass; Mezirow, J (1991) *Transformative Dimensions of Adult Learning*, San Francisco: Jossey Bass; Mezirow, J and associates (1990) *Fostering Critical Reflection in Adulthood: A guide to transformative and emancipatory learning*, San Francisco: Jossey Bass. I have also written on this topic for the distance educator; see Evans, T D (1991) 'An epistemological orientation to critical reflection in distance education', in Evans, T D and King, B (eds) *Beyond the Text: Contemporary writing on distance education*, Geelong: Deakin University Press, pp. 7–18.

Chapter 2

Learners' social and educational backgrounds

Adult learners come to their studies with social and educational backgrounds which provide important clues as to why they are studying and what they will learn from and do with their courses. Education and training are often portrayed as vehicles for self-improvement in material, social and intellectual ways. However, whether education and training are improving for learners or not depends substantially on the experiences and backgrounds they bring to bear on their courses, not just their existing knowledge and skills. It is conceivable that certain courses might even be counter-productive for some people if, for example, they experience failure or learn knowledge and skills which are, in particular ways, inferior to those they currently hold.

This chapter reflects a range of educational and social backgrounds which are presented by people studying different courses. The students' stories span different genders and generations, matters which are pursued specifically in Chapters 4 and 8, respectively. There are also observations made which span not only Australia and the United Kingdom, but also some other countries as these are reflected in the lives of the people involved. It is important to see the examples presented in this (and other) chapters as 'tips of the iceberg', not only in terms of the students in question, but especially in terms of student bodies in general.

On any particular course – especially if it attracts a large number of people, perhaps over several years – one can expect a range of backgrounds and experiences. These will vary as the social and historical circumstances unfold. Very little can be regarded as fixed when human beings are involved; indeed news and current affairs media make very considerable livings out the fact that there are daily and regular things to report and analyse. Within the dynamic nature of social worlds, it is possible to focus on particular instances and common attributes in order to make sense of what happens, and to influence what happens next. The following open and distance students' stories illustrate attempts to focus on the particular, and to identify the common, in the foundations upon which they build their learning.

Family and schooling: shaping learners

The earliest formal learning experiences which people have form a basis upon which their subsequent learning takes place. Attitudes and values about their learning, as well as the knowledge and skills with which they learn, have their roots in schooling. One of the difficulties for the open and distance educator is understanding what these roots were like for their students. For most adult students, schooling is something which they left behind several years ago, but it is also not uncommon to have students who have left school relatively recently and others whose school experiences were as much as several decades ago. However, schooling experiences themselves also vary and often this is connected to socio-economic background.

Mary's story:

> I was born in 1931, so I was brought up during the War years. Father was a coal miner and my mother didn't work. I was the eldest of three children. We had a very much working-class background. Like everyone else from our area in those days you just went to the local state school, it was just an ordinary school. I was one of the lucky ones to pass the scholarship, there weren't many in our days who did. It was considered unusual, I suppose, to pass the scholarship because people of my sort of background didn't really get very far. I went to a grammar school at the age of 11. My intended school was a girls' grammar school, but then they decided they were going to evacuate us to the country because of the Blitz. I was evacuated for two years and when it finished I came back and went to the girls' grammar school for two years. I had to leave the school at the age of 15 because my parents couldn't afford to keep me in school.

People such as Mary say that they see themselves as 'lucky' because they passed a scholarship to obtain a grammar school place, although the truth is probably that they were very capable at school and were able to make the best of their opportunities. George also was a child during the Second World War. His experiences of education and training were ones of failure and fear.

My school had been a hospital during the First World War and I think it was only used as a temporary kind of school for us. They have knocked it down now. My education was pretty basic. I think I have a learning problem. I might be dyslexic. Everything I say or read I reverse. So I didn't have a very good childhood in school. I didn't get on very well in school and I joined up with other boys of my own age who were in the same position and we went through school in the same way, not getting anywhere and creating as much havoc as we could. It was just elementary school. You had your 'Eleven Plus'[1] then you went to grammar school. My cousins went to grammar school, I was the only one in our family who didn't.

So I left school at 15 and got a job as an apprentice car mechanic, but I didn't do very well with that. I didn't seem to have the right aptitude. I tried to get myself an education because it was always said, especially by my mother, 'You must get yourself an education'. So then I went to night school. The other boys, apprentices and the like, would say, 'We don't want to go there'. We started in September and by the Christmas they would be bored and would be wandering around the streets instead of going to night school and of course, I was quite willing to join them. My mother got a letter from the headmaster saying, 'Your son hasn't been attending school', then there would be big rows in the house because they knew I should get on.

At 18 I did National Service in the Army. It was terrible. I was always behind, always last. You had to be first for everything. I arrived at the barracks. Imagine. I was marching down there from the station and there is this jail, honestly it looked like a jail, it frightened me to flaming death!

Basic training was right – my God it was basic! We were in the mountains in October. I could never keep up with anybody. Always it was physical. I always got the Bren gun magazine container – I was a weed of a boy, about 9 stone 5 lb – it must have weighed about a ton. The hills and mountains up there were terrible and they would make you carry these things up and down. It was really scary and I used to get quite frustrated.

I suppose I had a personality complex then; when anybody said anything to me I would overreact and fight. It was just second nature to me. I would use my fists instead of my tongue and being as I was a weedy little boy I always came off the worse, but it wouldn't stop me. I was always in trouble. The first six months I was on jankers (punishment duties). Especially when I went to Germany. For the first six months in Germany each month I had seven days jankers.

The misfortunes of war or the poor circumstances of families in both historical and current contexts can render people who would like to study unable to do so. For some, the thirst for learning persists so that, even many decades later, when courses become available to them through open and distance education approaches, they take the chance to slake their thirst. Despite George's difficulties with education and training, he obviously valued the point made by his family that 'you must get yourself an education'. He had worked his way through various training courses with the railways, post office and telephone services. At the time we spoke together, he had a degree – the testamatur was on the wall in the sitting room of his council house – which he had studied at a distance. He was continuing his studies to gain an honours degree.

Steve makes an interesting contrast to both Mary and George. He was of the next generation and started school in the 1960s:

My parents were both pharmacists with their own business. I went to the local primary school near where we lived which was in a pretty good area, really. Then I went to a private school. I sat an exam to get in, but it was a formality I suppose. I don't know if it was an actual entrance exam. I think people did fail, but I'm not sure. My parents could afford to send me there and they thought I could get a better education there. It was a Church of England school, all boys.

It is difficult for me to say whether I did have a better education. Looking back I don't really approve of what my parents did or the fact that I complied with it. I don't think very much of single-sex schools and I don't like the idea of private education. I went to university and I am now a pharmacist myself. One thing that higher education has given me is that I can appreciate the inequalities private education offers. From speaking to people, the opportunities I had were greater. Perhaps the teachers were better at the school I went to, rather than the teachers at the secondary school I would have gone to, but I find that difficult to believe. Perhaps the classes were smaller. Perhaps there were more opportunities to do examinations. I did ten O levels[2] which was normal for this school but the normal number at secondary schools was about eight, so I ended up with two more, not that that has had an effect on anything subsequently. I don't know whether the fact that I went to a private school has influenced anybody when I have actually used it for a job application.

In contrast to working-class Mary and George, Steve was a person who had inherited the fortunes of the middle class. His educational experiences were ones of seemingly automatic success. He took for granted the fact that he needed to continue his education in order to maintain his professional career as a pharmacist. However, he felt that as a pharmacist he was following uncritically in his parents' footsteps. So he enrolled in an arts course to broaden his knowledge and understanding and to do something which was of his own making.

For some people, schooling can be a very intense experience, as Mark explains of his childhood in Holland:

I went to primary school and then to a seminary. You were an intern, living with about 350 boys. It was basically a school set-up and run by a priest, with lay teachers as well. There was a big sleeping area and it was fairly Spartan. It was at the same time a grammar school and the major areas of education were six languages: Dutch, English, French, German and the classic Greek and Latin.

I never finished grammar school as such. After four years I came out, at 16. I came out and from a relatively protected environment – a male situation – I was just dumped right in the middle of Amsterdam in a business college, a trade college. I suppose they discovered I didn't have any vocation. I finished that in two years and then I went into a specialized management training college.

A seminary can be seen as 'closed' education institution. In Mark's case he seemed to leave with a mixture of resentment and yet strength of purpose. In more open education settings such people may 'blossom' or 'bust', depending on the care with which they are taught and advised.

For other people schooling can be almost non-existent, as was the case for Frances:

I hardly ever went to school, my parents didn't believe in it. They were terribly Bohemian and believed that what mattered was an enormous broadening experience in life. You were thrown right in at the deep end from the word go. I think it was partly because we had little money – my father was a parson – but we had a very principled background. From age 6 to 9 I was taught by my father, then I did go to a very good private school and then my parents took me away soon after. I think somebody in the parish paid for me because they were worried about me.

I read an enormous amount. By the time I was 12 I had read a lot of Tolstoy, including *War and Peace*. My father was a Latin and Hebrew scholar, so I did all that, but there was no mention of a formal education. When I was 10 it was decided that I ought to take the Eleven Plus, as it might be fun if I went to the local grammar school. That was the next experiment. I passed and then my father discovered that two girls at the school had become pregnant and so they decided not to send me. That year I had no education really at all and I think I was probably a bit of a mess, quite wild. I used to spend a lot of my time around the village and up trees. I had quite a fun upbringing in that sense, I suppose one could say.

I was supposed to have distance learning, because you have to fulfil certain educational things, but I suppose coming from a family where the parents could supply a lot of the education, there wasn't any great worry. I didn't do any education that year at all, I learned to drive a tractor at the age of 11 and milk a herd of 30 cows. I knocked around with my education a bit, they found a tutor for me, and I did a bit more of this and that and then they sent me to boarding school. They thought that perhaps I ought to have some kind of 'finishing off', so at 14 I went to boarding school for 18 months and it was an unmitigated disaster! In fact on one level I was more advanced than the girls I was with – it was a small private girls school, again paid for by a friend – and I was bored stiff on one level. I was enormously excited by maths. It was funny because the maths teacher had an affair with one of the girls. He was sacked and not replaced, so we then had no maths teaching at all. I asked if I could leave because I had enough of all this, so I left at 15 with no qualifications. I was half-way through my 'O level' course. I took the 'O levels' at home and got the ones in art subjects, but the science subjects I dropped, so I didn't get them.

Frances' experience contrasts markedly with Mark's. It is, perhaps, noteworthy that religion was behind both of their educational experiences, and their separations from mainstream education. In Frances' case, her experiences as a child mirror the sort of independent learning and local tuition which are often features of open and distance education. In Mark's case, his intense, almost total involvement with his school contrasts markedly with such features. However, it also has parallels with the sorts of involvement some open and distance education students experience at residential schools and weekend schools. In both Mark and Frances's cases, and those of George and Steve, their previous educational experiences were 'bitter-sweet' affairs. This seems typical of many adult students in that, although they often value education highly (otherwise they would probably not be studying), their experiences as learners have been both positive and negative. This demonstrates two important things which are relevant to the teacher or trainer. One is that learners can be remarkably resilient about their pursuit of education and the other is that they are not very resilient to education that they don't like. They may give up on a course, but this does not necessarily mean they will not seek out another in the future.

More generally, the students' stories in this section show the range of learning backgrounds the open and distance educator can encounter and needs to be able to address. Some learners may have left school several decades ago, some quite recently. Some may have left school at the minimum age – or not even have attended much at all, and others may be graduates or even postgraduates. Some may have learning difficulties, others may be accomplished independent learners. This list could be extended unendingly for as long as new learners' stories can be uncovered.

For learners, these stories show that their colleagues have highly disparate backgrounds and educational experiences such that they need not feel unusual themselves – being unusual is normal!

Learners' experiences as teachers

One of the often overlooked aspects of open and distance learners is that many of them have had experiences as teachers or trainers in some form. They may not be qualified school teachers, but rather occasional or regular instructors, coaches or trainers. Such experiences help shape their approaches to their own learning and also provide them with a certain acuity in viewing their open or distance education courses.

Michael is not a qualified teacher in the formal sense of being registered to practise in a school, but he is highly qualified in other ways and he depends on teaching for his living.

I was working for five years as a furniture removalist and I got interested in Karate. It was very involved, learning the Kata, blocks, moves, the language and so forth. After several years I earned my black belt, but I wanted to go further. I eventually chucked my job and went to Japan to study Karate. It was a big turn in my life, I knew it would be quite dramatic. When you go and train overseas against the Japanese, they have to prove they are the number one and so being a foreigner, to a certain degree, that made it difficult. It was quite hard, physically and mentally, I felt it really gave me strength for studying now.

When I came home I decided to set up my own school which I did in another city. I found a job as a storeman and packer and then I rented a Scout hall and started giving evening classes. After a while we decided to return here and try to get a Karate school going. I did all sorts of jobs to keep the money coming in so the school got established. Eventually I was able to make a full-time business for myself with my own school. I have been doing this for seven years now.

Michael has completed some small business oriented courses over the years and although he is very highly ranked in Karate, he continues to study Karate, often overseas. He left school in 1966 at age 16, with no qualifications, and obtained a job in an insurance office. This job involved evening study but he soon became bored and resigned to work as a removalist. Nineteen years after he left school he returned to night classes to complete the equivalent of his sixth form/year 12 examinations. He recalls:

I passed, then people in the night class said, 'We are going to university now'. It didn't even occur to me to do more studies. Someone suggested doing psychology and I thought that was interesting. I could see a connection between psychology and what I am teaching in Karate. In developing the mind and the self.

At the time we spoke he was in his third year of part-time study. His discipline learned through Karate, and his endeavours to teach others such discipline, gave him the motivation to learn and the strategies for coping with study which he lacked at school and for many of the years after he left.

Karen was another person who also turned the practice of her sport, rock climbing, into her living.

I was interested in biology. I did biology and chemistry in Matric,[3] English, maths 1 and maths 2, I was really hopeless at physics so I didn't like that. My father is a marine ecologist so I was interested in the sciences, but up until the end of high school I was interested in English and I enjoyed writing and thought I would be a writer. So I went to university and went into a BSc. The first year was a bit of a cruise except that I failed computing. I was just hopeless at computing for some reason. I have always been terrified of computers ever since then. I thought I would never get used to them but now I am writing a climbing guide book to a local mountain and I have had to use the computer and I reckon it is very different now.

First year I enjoyed, I really liked it a lot because it was a different lifestyle, it made a really big impact on me going to university instead of being at school, just as far as independence and freedom, new ideas and stuff. In second year I think I wasn't sure what I wanted to do with my science degree. I wasn't really sure what I wanted to be, where I wanted to end up, and so I wasn't motivated enough to continue to do all the work. So I dropped out and went on the dole. I did a bit of lab assistant work, met a guy that I became close to. He was a climber and so I went climbing with him and I've been addicted ever since.

I travelled a lot overseas and around Australia to go climbing. I then settled here because it has the best climbing. I started a rock climbing school for women out here, but that was only on weekends. I took people out to teach them how to climb for the weekend, give them a weekend course, women mostly. I teach anybody – men and women – who wants to climb, but I only advertised for women then because I perceived a need in the market for women to climb with women instructors. Some women prefer to climb with other women, and also there are lots of other climbing schools that cater for men, and there are none that cater specifically for women.

My costs were really minimal because I had enough equipment myself. I mostly advertised by word of mouth, but I did have a few little expenses. I think I put out a few pamphlets and things around the shops, the climbing shops, a few notices. I can't remember how many people I got in the first year, normally I would take out groups of two if possible, two or three. Then when I went to Europe a friend of mine carried on the work for me. I taught climbing in Germany for a bit, cash in hand, and then I returned here to carry on my work.

Karen's experiences as an instructor (including developing a climbing guide book) rekindled her interest in her own learning. She enrolled in an arts degree at a distance which she felt would help her understand more about women and society, and writing, all of which her previous science education had omitted.

Both Michael and Karen show how their confidence, gained through competence in essentially physical activities, flowed into their confidence and self-esteem as learners. There is, perhaps, a case to be made for people who wish to do well at their learning to keep themselves physically fit through regular exercise and a good diet. Certainly, adult students invariably have to mix a variety of responsibilities with their studies – as is demonstrated in subsequent chapters – and they may well be better able to withstand the physical demands of studying for long hours when assignments or exams are due, or when attending demanding residential schools, if they are physically fit. However, what Karen and Michael also exude is a mental confidence and resilience which their sports have helped them develop. A sport which not only develops physical fitness, but which also helps people explore their physical and mental limits, may have additional benefits for the 'loneliness of the long distance student'.

Returning to the theme of learners' experiences as teachers, not everyone enjoys their period on the other side of the teaching–learning divide. William spent 24 years in the Royal Navy, ending his career as a Chief Petty Officer.

> I was posted at one stage as an instructor with the boys. A shore-based job. It is good being ashore for a while, but instructing was not really my cup of tea. I then did a period training people in air direction, training radar people. That's all gone now.

> You were drafted in to instruct and it wasn't really what I'd joined the Navy to do. Sometimes there are proper Education Officers on the ships, or someone such as the Met Officer doubles up, giving classes and overseeing exams and such. When I was ordered to an instructors' posting or had to do some of it alongside my regular duties, I wasn't keen on the idea. I didn't really fancy it.

William's response to his periods as both a trainer and learner in the Navy was that this was utilitarian stuff which was behind him. He was now working in another job and enjoying his studies for his own benefit. The impression was that he did not care about those who were not interested in learning (such as dragooned cadets) and he was only interested in being taught by tutors who cared about their subjects and were not (just) tutoring for the money.

Others, such as Rod, are keen on teaching as an art and craft for its own sake. He is a qualified teacher and was employed for some years in that profession. He worked subsequently on developing curriculum materials for a training authority and then decided to branch out by himself.

I've been qualified as a driving instructor for years, I used to do a fair bit. I was doing it full-time sometimes during the summer school holidays. I have now just recently got a decent car with dual controls fitted, so that I am only doing that part-time, but that gives me opportunity to expand or contract, depending on how the other work goes. I have got the small holding which I am learning about farming – both from courses, field days, etc., as well as experientially, on-the-job – and which I enjoy. It has got room for greater development, but involves risk capital for any future great development so that I don't like to expand it too much.

I also bought the village school when it closed which I run basically as a community centre. I enjoy it very much. I organize courses there. I don't actually run most of the courses myself. We offer anything and everything. I also do a bit of private tuition, mainly maths, which keeps me amused! I thoroughly enjoy these activities because I can keep all of them small scale and so I never get bored. There is always a variety. It does have difficulties because you are trying to keep everyone happy. You are at one job and people will ring you up and ask you particular points of something that happened four weeks ago. I am trying to remember various facts on completely varying topics.

Rod is an example of a person for whom education and training are interwoven throughout his life; he can be seen to be practising what is often termed 'lifelong learning'. The concept of 'lifelong learning', at first glance, conveys a notion of a linear educational thread stretched through a lifetime; however, what Rod displays is a complexity of educational threads woven into a tapestry. He shows that there are typically teaching, instructing, training, coaching, tutoring and other 'teacherly' threads interwoven over a lifetime with learner, trainee, student, tutee and other 'learnerly' threads. As the above few examples show, adult learners are often educators (in some form) and they learn to teach, as well as teach to learn.

In this chapter a few examples from the experiences and backgrounds of students illustrate that there is a rich diversity in adult students which presents the educator with multiple dilemmas. This is especially the case for distance educators (and some open educators who rely on highly developed materials, packages and software) who are used to preparing their courses well in advance of knowing who their students are in name, let alone in nature. How can one design for diversity? Open educators who use, for example, negotiated curriculum, reflexive teaching or critical pedagogies in (predominantly) face-to-face, or (maybe) computer-mediated interactive contexts, have certain advantages, both for hearing students' voices, needs and interests and in being able to respond to them. But it looks, from the brief glimpse of learners' lives which has been afforded here, as if recognizing the potential effects of the educational threads educators spin on the patterns of learners' educational tapestries is an important foundation. In subsequent chapters the patterns become even richer!

Notes

1 An examination taken at age 11 (hence, 'Eleven Plus') to determine whether children could go to grammar schools. Approximately 20–30 per cent of children went to grammar schools. Grammar schools provided the opportunity of schooling through to sixth form and, thence, into university or college for those who obtained the highest grades (see note 3). Those who failed their 'Eleven Plus' generally went to secondary modern or technical schools if they remained within the state education system. Such schools usually catered for children through to fourth form and, thence, into work or apprenticeships, rather than full-time education.

2 'O levels' refers to what were known as General Certificate of Education Ordinary Level examinations taken in England and Wales at the end of fifth form (Year 11). A (Advanced) level examinations were usually taken after a further two years in sixth form and provided the gateways to higher education.

3 'Matric' refers to matriculation exams which were sixth form/Year 12 examinations in Australia which served similar purposes (principally selection for higher education) to the A level exams in England and Wales (see note 2).

Chapter 3

Money: coping with the costs of study

Unlike other government services – such as health, welfare, law and order – virtually everyone in developed nations is required to use education services for at least ten years of their early lives. In fact, the majority of members of the rising generation of young people in such nations are likely to spend 12 or 13 years at school, followed by a few more years of full-time or part-time education or training. In developing nations, the development of primary and secondary school systems is usually amongst the highest priorities. While most people hope to avoid using medical practitioners, lawyers, nurses, police officers or dentists for anything other than routine requirements, these same people actively make enormous demands on their teachers. It is even seen as positive to pursue education as far as possible, whereas pursuing as much time as possible as a patient either in a hospital or in a dentist's chair would be seen as quite weird! In two weeks at school, young people spend about the same amount of time with teachers as they would with dentists in their whole lifetime.

This enormous social and individual commitment to education and training – in both developed and developing societies – represents equivalent state, community and personal investments of financial, resource and human kinds. The previous chapter provided a glimpse of the differences in social backgrounds that adult learners exhibit when they present themselves for further study through open and distance education. An element of these backgrounds concerns the differences in the financial wealth which their families were able to bring to bear during their upbringing. Now, as adult learners, they confront the responsibilities of finding their own means of meeting the costs of study. Although money is at the heart of such means and costs, it is not the entirety. Demands on time, competing family and work responsibilities, etc., make for other important means and costs which adult students have to balance in order to study. Subsequent chapters in this book deal with these and related matters so, in this chapter, the financial cost of study is the principal focus.

Historically, open and distance education institutions have usually been established by governments to provide education which is accessible to people from a variety of locations, circumstances and backgrounds, largely irrespective of their capacities to pay. This is not to say that the education provided has been free, indeed this is rarely the case, but it is usually heavily subsidized by the state so that the actual price paid by students is a small proportion of the real costs of providing the service. More recently, approaches from open and distance education have been employed by emerging education and training enterprises to provide full-fee services – either direct to the learners or though employers or other agencies – which return a profit. Such enterprises are not new, indeed the history of distance education is interwoven with correspondence education enterprises and state subsidized correspondence education institutions. What is new is the burgeoning of such enterprises which occurs alongside broader technological shifts. Such shifts provide both the demand for specific courses to learn the new technologies and also the capacities to produce and distribute courses with greater quality and efficiency.[1]

Within any national economy[2] the costs of education need to be met by the various parties involved. Typically, the state absorbs most of the costs and meets these out of its taxation and other revenue. The balance of the costs is met by the students, their sponsors (employers, scholarships, etc.) and by any foundations, bequests, earnings, grants, sponsorships, etc. which the institutions obtain. For further education (such as trade and vocational certificate and diploma courses), and higher education (that is, undergraduate and postgraduate degree courses) in particular, it is more usual to find that the student is expected to pay a greater proportion of the total costs of education than is the case with schooling. Thus, for example, in many countries, such as in North America, the costs of further and higher education are borne more heavily by the student. In others, such as most European nations and Australia and New Zealand, the state has assumed more of the costs. In recent years, the expansion of demand for further and higher education has led to most nations trying to increase the amount of money they recoup from the students.

The increase in 'user-pays' approaches to the funding of open and distance education does conflict with at least some of their intentions, such as access and, indeed, this conflict has applied over much of the history of distance education. The previous chapter demonstrated that some older people were only able to obtain further or higher education when the opportunities provided by open and distance education occurred much later in their lives. For younger people, educational expectations, opportunities and access were generally greater during their formative years. These expectations, together with the demands of commerce and industry for a more highly educated workforce, have contributed substantially to the boom in all forms of education, especially in open and distance education. The various attempts to reorganize the funding arrangements to cope with the demand means that many students have to make important decisions about the money they will need to spend in order to obtain the open or distance education they require.

Feeling the pinch: coping with increasing course fees

If students are confronted with increased course costs imposed by government or institutions during their courses, then there are predictable and understandable responses. Of course, it is virtually impossible to ascertain the opinions of those unknown numbers of people who exclude any consideration of returning to study because of mass media and other reports they receive about the introduction of higher fees and charges. Those who are already studying feel powerless to do anything about the charges other than withdraw from their studies or pay the money. As the following comments show, there is considerable disaffection when increased costs are imposed mid-course. Karen, who is the rock-climber introduced in the previous chapter, lives on a very modest income. She was very unhappy about a new government fee she had incurred.[3]

> I am really violently against this fee because I think it really stinks. It really sucks having to pay this fee, particularly when it isn't means tested. At the time I was averaging less than if I had been on the dole, and to have to pay this administration fee really sucked.

> If you were on the dole you didn't have to pay. So if I had been registered and receiving unemployment benefits I would have been exempt. But I wanted to support myself rather than be on the dole.

Karen also spoke out strongly about the new way of calculating and charging fees, to be introduced the following year, which included a means test element.[4]

> Well the proposed scheme for me that is more acceptable purely from a selfish point of view. It is a graduation tax, so you don't have to pay until you finish, I think. I don't really intend to graduate, so that is going to be so far down the road I don't even think about it.

> I mean I am totally against it. I think basically it stinks, but because it is more acceptable to the community at large, it is the sort of thing that is going to get through. It is more acceptable because it is only charging people whose income is over a certain level to start with, and so it is not seen to be directly discriminatory against the unemployed, dependent women, people on pensions. The Government has put in this lure that there will be so many more hundreds of places in universities because of it. Basically I think it is a pretty cynical exercise by the Government. I mean, just the fact that higher education has been free or basically free since the mid-70s now to bring a charge on it, seems to me to be going backwards. I think it is a retrogressive step.[5]

Marilyn found that the increase in charges she experienced on her journalism course was reasonable for her circumstances. As a young journalist she was not earning a lot of money, but she found herself able to cope.

> I think the new charge will certainly disadvantage some, yes. I think this new HECS tax system is better than a flat fee. The flat fee would have been difficult for a lot of people, such as people studying at home as an interest.

Damien is a telephone switchboard operator and was annoyed by the new charges.

> I deferred for a year because I wasn't going to pay the original charge. I paid this year but I wasn't going to. I couldn't make up my mind whether I would do any more study, and I thought in my mind if enough people weren't studying then they might reject the whole idea, so I deferred for a year and just enjoyed the year watching videos and doing nothing. I still don't like the new charge. I mean the first great incentive for me not to do any more study was the charge.

Damien wondered whether, if enough people refused to re-enrol due to the new charges, the Government would rescind its decision. However, the demand for places was such that, although there was a drop in applications for some courses, this merely reduced the numbers turned away. The consequence of the imposition of the new charge and of Damien's reaction to it was that he inflicted the penalty on himself. He lost a year of his education which he then decided to regain later. It is difficult to know how students such as Damien could be advised about the consequences of their decisions. Increases in charges, especially when they are imposed nationally by a government, are often contested by various groups, including students' organizations. Part of the contest may be to promote a boycott of courses, but such collective actions are difficult to organize and effect in distance education, or in part-time study more generally. However, as was discussed at the beginning of this chapter, they also have to account for the fact that, eventually, someone has to pay for the courses.

Stephanie's position was a little different. She seemed to agree with the charge but did not like the way it was being imposed because she feared she may have to pay it!

I propose to do the second unit next year but, as far as I am concerned, it is a little bit up in the air with the money situation, with the things the Government is bringing in. The tax on income is the main thing that worries me.

I don't mind paying for what I am doing. I actually said that to someone today. I have been brought up with that attitude. My father paid for the first part of my university education and I know, as a taxpayer, all of this education has to be paid for. But I do resent the fact that the Government wants to tax you once your income level reaches a certain stage because I am in the position that I am a partner in the farm and we share our income so my assessment of income is actually on what my husband is earning, on the farm. But the income isn't anything I am earning from what I am doing as far as my course is concerned. It is my husband's work on the farm and if I am going to be taxed on that for my course I can't really see that it is very fair. I think maybe it is something we will have to discuss with the accountant, whether it will be feasible for me to go on and do it next year. Which is really a sad thing.

Stephanie's anguish was partly to do with the conflict between her principle that she ought to be paying and her reluctance in practice to do so. Presumably, Stephanie and her husband were splitting their incomes in order to minimize their total tax. In which case, Stephanie was wanting 'to have her cake and eat it too'! Eventually, she did continue her course. As she had four children for which she was receiving an allowance from the Government, it seems likely that she wouldn't have been required to pay for the foreseeable future.

Nina found the whole matter of the new charges and how they were to be administered and collected confusing, but she was persevering.

> I don't really understand it all. They sent me the great blurbs on it. I read one letter and thought, 'I will work it out and if it sounds too much in the end I'll give it away'. I haven't really thought about the money part but if I really want to study then I will do without a few other things. You weigh out your priorities. Your money priorities.

Anne, however, had decided to limit her aspirations as a result of the increased costs of study.

> Before they talked about the tertiary tax I was quite determined to do a Masters, but having done these three units this semester I don't think I want to incur any more costs. I wanted to do a Masters because I have taken very strongly to the policy area. I was going to do a course work Masters in policy studies.

> I am philosophically opposed to taxes which are selectively applied and I think it is grossly unfair to people in my situation where, apart from the first year, I have always supported my education. Now I am to be taxed on the basis of the earnings which I have acquired without having a tertiary qualification. I resent paying a tax on my income based on the fact that I have achieved it without that.

Anne's work in the public service meant that she had seen that a degree would help her obtain more responsible positions. Arguably, a Masters degree in policy studies would have helped her even further. However, the loss would not just be Anne's. Her employer would also lose the potential of someone with a higher degree.

One of the points which stands out from these students' reactions to charges is that the students appear to be very cost-sensitive, even to the extent that they will set aside the potential intrinsic and extrinsic gains of continuing their education because of the increased costs they will incur. There is evidence here that eventually some students, like Damien and Stephanie, return to study as they adjust to the idea of having to pay more.

It is perhaps not surprising how people view their own circumstances as being of the type which should exclude them from payment. People who run courses should not be surprised at either the protest they are likely to receive when substantial fee increases are levied or at the variety of circumstances which are likely to be used to gain exemptions if they are available. Students should also recognize that if they are embarking on a protracted period of study, rather than a short training course, then there are clear possibilities for fees and other charges to be increased. For those who are likely to encounter difficulties should such increases occur, there are often strategies which can be employed to minimize the costs or to meet them. The next sections provide some ideas from students in this regard.

Balancing the books: paying for learning resources and activities

The costs of study extend well beyond the tuition fees and other charges which students have to pay. The purchase of learning materials – from pens and paper, through books and calculators, to videocassette recorders and computers – is not something which students take lightly. Likewise, the costs incurred in attending tutorials, practicals, examinations and residential schools are often ones which weigh heavily on a family's or individual's income. The earnings which people may have to forgo to participate in education and training can be significant. Mario was undergoing a company training scheme which involved him attending classes as well as studying independently at home.

> I used to work whatever overtime that was available. I still do a bit, but what with study it is too difficult. Some of the hours I could put in after work I now have to attend the classes or go to the training centre to use the computer. I don't really mind because it is for my benefit as well as the company's. Overtime was getting tight anyway, but we could still do with the money. Who couldn't?

The loss of earnings for learners may generally be a minor concern because attributing direct loss of income to studying is difficult. Even in Mario's case, it would be difficult to apply a precise figure because it is impossible to know what overtime would have been available for him and how much he would have been able or willing to undertake. Clearly, there would be a loss of income in his case; something which may well be offset by eventual higher earnings as a result of a job regrading or promotion based on his completed training and associated work performance.

The actual costs of study in terms of the payments made by students are easier to determine, although it is unusual for people within educational organizations to assess the total costs to students. Teachers and trainers tend to see the books and other materials they prescribe for students to buy only in terms of their own course and not the whole award or programme which the learner is following. It is also the case that if the teacher or trainer *recommends* a book or resource (and sometimes this may even just be a passing positive reference in a training session, tutorial or course material), then some students believe that their learning will be directly enhanced if they obtain (or conversely they will be disadvantaged if they do not) the book or resource in question. It is incumbent on educators to make the status of their recommendation clear and for learners to verify their interpretations before making a purchase. Learners can easily do this by asking where the recommended resources will be useful directly and indirectly in their studies. For some workplace-based courses, learning materials and resources are provided, if not to each individual student as a loan or acquisition, then in a central location where they may be used or borrowed. But most students in open and distance education obtain their learning materials at their own expense.

Nina, as with most students in developed nations, had a videocassette recorder before she enrolled and so could make use of the supplementary videos on her course. Books, however, had to be bought.

> Yes, I have a video which is quite handy. I can send for a videocassette they had, next year I might try and get more of them. I bought books through the second-hand bookshop and I think I have learnt my lesson there. I think one I opened once. I think I would be better off trying to borrow them from the library. They must have class sets I suppose. I was pretty lucky because I had some books anyway so that didn't worry me. I think it would add up over the years if I bought every book, especially when you don't really use that much out of them.

As a retired person, Amy had to be careful about her expenditure. She enrolled in a course which involved some quite expensive books.

> It could have been quite a lot of expense to buy everything on my course. There are a lot of books set. A friend did the course last year and she has lent me a lot of the books I need. I have covered them with brown paper

wrapping so that they go back to her tidy when I have finished at the end of the year. I don't regret money spent on things, but I have to be careful.

Amy demonstrates the sort of careful cost control that one often expects with people of her age (she is in her 70s). It is not just that they are older and on smaller incomes or pensions, but often, as was recounted in the previous chapter, they have been through much harder times during their childhood and early adulthood and have learned lessons in economizing not generally learned by subsequent generations.

David noted that the price of two of the books he was required to buy did not seem to reflect good value for money in terms of the printing costs, if not the content.

> Well, there are two here when I look at them I think 'Oh God' what I have spent on them! But apart from that the other books are all quite modest really. These ones were very expensive and one of them was a paperback. I thought at least it would have hard covers for the price.

Teachers and trainers in open and distance education are often confronted with difficult decisions about setting books for their courses. Once courses are developed around particular books it is very costly to change the course materials if a book is unavailable or becomes too expensive. This is particularly a problem with imported books for which the reliability of supply and price increases become more unpredictable. For those in developing nations the problems are magnified further as shipping schedules are less frequent and the acquisition of foreign currency for purchasing is usually more difficult, erratic and expensive. The purchase and use of non-print resources can be even worse, especially if electricity is necessary for their use.[6] For most students in developed nations, the costs are ones which they are willing to bear for useful materials, as Marilyn exemplifies.

> It hasn't really been a problem. I suppose I have a relatively healthy bank balance so I have been able to write out cheques for books and that sort of thing.

But in distance education and some open education courses, students incur substantial postage and telephone costs to send assignments, communicate with their tutors, etc. Karen explains,

> I would spend $100 in postage and maybe $100–$150 that I would spend on books and materials.[7] So to me it is worth it.

Karen's view of buying books and paying for her postage costs, contrasts markedly with the strident opposition she exhibited in her quoted remarks in the previous section on paying the new government charges for her education. It seems that most students see it as being fair and reasonable that they should buy (useful) books, particularly as they appreciate obtaining something tangible. The 'tangible assets' argument does not apply to the postage charges Karen was willing to pay. Again, students seem happy to pay what they expect to incur at the outset (such as postage for assignments), especially if these are things that they have expected to pay for in their previous education, even during their schooling.

Attending tutorials, exams, practicals, residential schools and so forth usually presents additional costs for students which are far from inconsequential. In Chapters 6 and 7 some of the time-related costs are discussed; in this section the monetary costs of participating in such activities will be considered. As seen before, some students are quite resourceful in keeping their costs to a minimum. Nina uses her friends in the city to help reduce accommodation costs for weekend schools.

> It is a great cost if you have to go down town all the time. We are lucky we have got someone there we can stay with. This also gives us another reason to travel down there. Otherwise it would be a bit expensive and, what with the fees, I don't know what would happen.

Sometimes students have the choice of whether they attend tutorials, etc., or not. This has the advantage of leaving the decision to the students and not ruling out of the course itself those who, for whatever reasons, are unable to attend. However, if open education is meant to be available to all those who wish to enrol, then the monetary cost of voluntary attendance is something which effectively removes the choice from those who have insufficient money to attend. The requirement to attend may have been removed by the institution, but the choice is also removed by the cost. This presents itself as a dilemma for most open and distance educators: every optional tuition activity created contains with it the potential to discriminate against those who are already disadvantaged. The more worthwhile the activity, the worse the consequences of the discrimination. There are many powerful educational reasons for offering a variety of ways to enhance students' learning experiences, but the dilemma doesn't disappear. The same sort of dilemma also occurs outside of monetary considerations. Perhaps the most obvious is where those with particular disabilities are further discriminated against as a consequence of being unable to attend tuition sessions by virtue of their disability.

Obviously, most educators develop and offer tuition and other activities which are priced within the means of the majority of students. David found this to be the case for his residential school. He was prepared to pay and then was advised that his local council might well assist with his expenses.

It was something that was said on the course that one should try and ask the local council for assistance. I just rang through to the council offices and said I am attending residential school for my course and asked if they could help. They said 'Yes, as long as you can prove that you had been there we will pay it'. They paid it, I sent them my certificate of attendance and they paid up. I can't remember how much it was for travelling, but I got that as well.

Paul had a similar experience. He had to pay for some of his course, but eventually his employer helped with the costs.

They paid 80 per cent of my course fees, books. They wouldn't pay for the first year, I had to pay for that myself, to prove I could do it. Once I did that they have paid for everything since. I also get help with my petrol costs and running costs to attend the tutorials. It isn't much, but it helps.

Clearly, for some students the costs of study are not necessarily those they actually spend on their books and travel, etc. Some are able to obtain full or partial reimbursements at a later stage. It often helps those who are advising students on trying to 'balance the books' for their study to know what possibilities there are in order to help students in need or to help those with entitlements to pursue their various options. It is also worthwhile for students to ask their employer, local authority, or other potentially useful agencies what help may be available. Their tutors, training officers, counsellors, etc. may also be able to provide useful advice on 'balancing the books'. The next section addresses the related issue of finding funds for study.

Finding funds

Finding the money to pay for courses is something which any adult student needs to consider. There are many learners who assume the entire student-component cost of their courses. In effect, as was noted previously, the tuition costs are often subsidized by the state or other authorities. However, as has also been shown, the sum of the costs of the student fee, books and other learning resources, travel and tuition expenses, can be of concern to many. Of course, it must be stated that the students' comments provided in this chapter are exactly that: comments from students. Therefore, they exclude comments from those who could not afford the costs of study and never enrolled in the first place. It is difficult to estimate the exact costs of open and distance education courses for students. Some courses, especially full-fee courses in business fields, can be very expensive. Those courses where there is some subsidy by government, business or other organizations, cost a few hundred pounds Sterling or several hundred dollars in North America or Australasia. To this must be added the course materials and other costs noted in the previous section. In total, the costs are significant and do act as a deterrent for some. For others, there are ways of obtaining assistance with their costs. In this section some of the students' ways of finding funds are recounted.

In the previous section, Paul, who works for a government department, explained that he commenced studying largely at his own expense, but that he eventually obtained substantial financial support from his employer. This support came after he had 'proved himself' in the first year and it was based on some assessment of the worth of the course to his work. This is not uncommon in both the private and the public sector. It is a major source of assistance for those who are in work and who are completing a course, of their own choice, but which enhances their career and job prospects and performance.

Rod, who had been a school teacher for some years and was now largely self-employed, pointed out that he found that different government employing authorities had different policies on paying for teachers' further studies.

The letter the local authority wrote back said they will not consider payment for any qualified teachers.

You will find that nearly all the teachers in the town schools have a three-year qualification, and they have been teaching for up to 25 years. To be honest they are all very good teachers, mature teachers, who are particularly experienced in their profession. I cannot understand why the local authority will not pay for them to complete their fourth year and get a BEd. They need training more than anybody else, don't they?

The original point I was making was when I was in my previous local authority everything was paid for. All your fees and residential schools were paid for. Travelling to tutorials and residential schools and that sort of thing.

Rod's experience as someone who was no longer employed by an organization or authority willing to help was that finding the funds for study was very hard.

It will be disappointing for me because I can't go on with my course as far as I can see at the moment, on an economic basis. A drawback to living in rural areas is who pays for the courses? This is a lovely area to live in because it is remote and has few people, but this means the local authority has less money. Therefore they are very reluctant to pay, especially as I am a qualified teacher. They will pay half of some courses for some people. It is a big factor, especially when you consider the low incomes of this area. There should be more grants here, not necessarily out of the rates. The majority of the people are on atrociously low wages and couldn't afford courses to help themselves and the area.

There are multiple dilemmas faced by government authorities in these circumstances, especially if open education is something which is valued. A teacher – even one who is three-year, rather than four-year, trained as is often the contemporary standard – will be highly educated in comparison with the general population. Therefore, in a case such as Paul's, a government authority could well argue that their expenditure should go to those who have received less education during their lifetime. But the ways in which individuals' needs and their potential to contribute to the community are assessed raise complex issues. Open education organizations, and arguably distance education ones as well, probably could make useful representations to government authorities on such matters, in terms of both individual cases and policy formation.

Some students are of an age where they are not looking to education to enhance their employment prospects or careers, but are studying for their own interests and at their own expense. Amy is a retired person who lives off her pension and superannuation. As was noted earlier in this chapter, when possible, she also borrowed books from previous students to keep her costs down. The costs of fees were difficult for her to meet but she found a solution.

I pay for the course through the bank, monthly, they do that. I spread it over the eight months or rather seven months it is really. I pay two eighths and then eighths each month if you see what I mean. I pay a quarter of it first and then the rest is paid in instalments, so I don't really notice it.

For people on low incomes, it is often important to have the opportunity to spread the payments associated with their learning. A commercial arrangement with a bank, negotiated by the institution, or a government underwritten scheme, such as one which defers payments through the income taxation system, can make the difference between people enrolling in courses or not, or withdrawing from courses or not. Students often do not know, or are embarrassed to ask, about means of spreading payments or of obtaining assistance. Open education should be 'open' to providing advice and assistance on such matters, and students should feel that they are entitled to feel 'open' about asking.

A 'traditional' means of finding the funds for education has been for the (young) learner to be supported financially by their parents. However, with adult students this becomes something which is either less available as both parties age, or is less acceptable as they establish their independence. Marilyn found that she was having to assume the responsibilities for her own education at a time when the costs were increasing.

Well I was fortunate last year because my parents paid the charge for me so that was a consideration. Now when my income reaches $22,000 I am going to be taxed extra for my education fees. But I thought that if I want to succeed – when I get the degree it will help promotion or with getting a job then it is probably worth it. I have always wanted to go on campus to university – living on campus would be great. But I think it is a shame that education is becoming something for higher class, or élite, or wealthier people.

Marilyn was able to claim against her income tax for her journalism course because it was a work–related course.

I think they worked out to be – just from my taxation return – I claimed everything for my study costs as they are work-related. That included travel to orientation day, returning library books, stationery, all that sort of thing. Any study expenses which are work-related over a certain amount each year you can claim.

Depending on the income tax laws which apply, this can be an appropriate way for some students on job-related courses to receive some rebate for their expenses. However, some taxation systems do not permit this or the guidelines are complicated or strict. In such circumstances it is useful if students can be alerted to the possibilities and limitations, and also be provided with the information which will enable them to obtain appropriate documentation from the educational organization, their employer, taxation office, etc. Organizations involved in education and training could also lobby their governments on enhancing the possibilities for students in this regard.

Karen's strong views against the increased charges she incurred were given previously and these contrasted with her subsequent views on the money she paid for the other costs of her study, such as books, postage and materials. As a low-income person she had calculated what she needs to do to obtain the money to study. She said previously,

> I would spend $100 in postage and maybe, I don't know, $100 – $150 on books and materials.

She continued,

> As I am instructing climbing I will earn that in two days. So to me it is worth it. As I am on a low income I can last on something like bread and cheese if I have to. If I really want to get something then I will work and scrimp for it.

> I am not really living on the breadline as such. I have got savings, so it is not like I have got to pay fees or books or something next week and what am I going to do? It is like I do have money in the bank, it is just that I don't spend very much, so when the bills come in I have got a bit of reserve, yes. It is not desperate on a low-income lifestyle, if you have a low-income expenditure.

Karen's position, which has surfaced at various points in this chapter, demonstrates some of the apparent contradictions which occur when students confront the costs of their study. It seems that a lot depends on their expectations of costs and their previous experiences. If they have been used to paying for particular aspects of their studies, especially where they accept these knowingly when they apply for their courses, then these are generally coped with. Where costs are added without consent or warning during study, then students may withdraw, resist or grudgingly accept the bills.

In this chapter the focus has tended to be on those for whom finding the funds for their learning is a concern or a problem. For some students the costs are not a problem because such costs are either low or paid by an employer or other party, or they have more than sufficient income or wealth to meet the costs. Before enrolling, most students are in financial positions where the costs of study need to be understood within the context of their personal or family budgets. Open and distance educators and their organizations can assist, not only by providing appropriate information on costs, but also by being sensitive to the difficulties some students may experience (often temporarily), and by providing advice and strategies to help them cope.

Notes

1 For a discussion of the relationships between technologies and education, especially in terms of open and distance education, see, Evans, T D and Nation, D E (1993) 'Educational technologies: reforming open and distance education', in Evans, T D and Nation, D E (eds) *Reforming Open and Distance Education: Critical reflections from practice*, London: Kogan Page, pp. 196–214; Evans, T D and Nation, D E (1993) 'Distance education, educational technology and open learning: converging futures and closer integration with conventional education', in Nunan, T (ed.) (1993) *Distance Education Futures: Selected papers from the 11th Biennial Forum of the Australian & South Pacific Association for Distance Education*, Adelaide: University of South Australia, pp. 15–35.

What is unclear from the technological reformations underway in education is the impact on costs, not only on changes to capital and recurrent costs and who meets them, but also especially the distribution of costs between, say, learners and their institutions, or between government and industry.

2 The education 'business' – along with other aspects of contemporary societies – is becoming more internationalized in both its economic and political operations. For the purposes of the argument here, I have framed the discussion as if a national economy were where all the costs of an educational institution are met. The same general argument can be mounted in terms of international educational trade and aid, but setting out such an argument would become unnecessarily clouded by geo-political and ideological differences.

3 At the time Karen was interviewed, the Australian government had

imposed an 'administration fee' on all university students, irrespective of study load or income. This fee was replaced by a much more sophisticated Higher Education Contribution Scheme (HECS). Under HECS, all students incur a liability equivalent to a proportion (about 20 per cent) of the average per capita costs of educating people in higher education. This liability is met by them through the income taxation system when their taxable income exceeds a threshold figure roughly equivalent to the minimum wage. There is also an option of paying the HECS charge 'up front' (minus a discount) when enrolling each year or semester. This procedure for collecting revenue from the 'users' of education has attracted international attention by governments and policymakers, for example, by the United Kingdom government in 1992 and by the vice-chancellors (presidents) of universities in the (British) Commonwealth countries at their meeting in Wales in 1993.

Returning to Karen's story, in effect, she was complaining about a fee that she had paid on enrolment which represented about one quarter of her subsequent liability under HECS. However, she was on a low income, and she would not have had to meet this liability until such time as she earned more than the threshold income.

4 See note 3 above for details. Karen actually misunderstood several aspects of the (then) proposed scheme; however, she exhibits the sorts of misunderstandings an actual or potential student might construct about such schemes, especially ones as sophisticated as that proposed (and enacted) by the Australian government. Clearly, it is in organizations' interests to ensure that they provide clear and accessible advice to actual or potential students.

5 Higher education tuition fees were abolished in Australia by the Whitlam Labor Government in 1973. This had been a significant pledge made during the campaign which led, in December 1972, to the election of the first Labor government for 23 years. For people like Karen, the absence of fees was an article of faith. The introduction of fees by the Hawke Labor government 16 years later was seen by such people as a breach of this faith.

6 Kwasi Ansu-Kyeremeh has pointed out from his research in Ghanaian villages, that even the purchase of dry cell batteries for audiocassette players (there being no reticulated electricity) can be impossible due to the costs and the vagaries of imported supplies. See Ansu-Kyeremeh, K (1991) 'Distance education in a developing context: Ghana', in Evans, T D and King, B (eds) *Beyond the Text: Contemporary writing on distance education*, Geelong, Deakin University Press, pp. 137–51. In contrast to

'developed' countries, the ubiquity and reliability of, for example, electricity and telecommunications, cannot be generally assumed.

7 At the time of writing, A$100 represents about £47 Sterling or US$71.

Chapter 4

Sex: learning in gendered worlds

In order to understand learners it is necessary to recognize the gendered nature of the learners themselves, of their contexts, of the education they encounter, and of the meaning frameworks which are brought to bear in understanding social worlds. Understanding gender is not about recognizing that matters of 'balance' between the sexes are important, or about expunging sexist language and practices from courses, important though these may be. Rather, understanding gender concerns recognizing the power and depth of masculine and feminine meanings and practices in our culture. These meanings and practices are constructed and reconstructed through each rising generation so that, while changes and modifications are made and adopted, the gendering processes continue with vigour.

Education has had a mammoth part to play in gendering social worlds, not only through what is taught, but also through how it is taught. Educational organizations also reap what they (and others) sow; thereby, they confront the products and outcomes of gendering processes in the demands that are put upon them, through the people they employ and the students they enrol. As with many social problems, gender inequalities are seen as being, at least partly, solved through education. In particular, open and distance education have been nominated in many societies as key means of providing educational opportunities for women who have been previously disadvantaged. Such educational opportunities, once taken, are then believed to provide better access to the workplace and more career options therein. As with most, if not all, things concerned with social inequalities, open and distance education's contributions have been mixed, due mainly to the complexity of forces at work. This chapter explores some of the complexities and contradictions of gender in open and distance education through some students' stories.

'Housewives' Choice': women returning to study

In so-called 'traditional family' circumstances, women absorb the majority of the responsibilities for domestic work and childrearing. A variety of social and economic changes in recent decades has dented this tradition so that women have been encouraged to see themselves in terms of economic contributors to society (and breadwinners for the family) and as necessary participants throughout the social and political structures. To a lesser degree, men have been encouraged to see themselves as having responsibility for domestic work and childrearing. Active participation in social, political and economic structures invariably requires high levels of educational attainment and, therefore, women have seen that they need to avail themselves of education and training if they are not only to move out of the home as their 'occupation', but also to work in positions which require more than basic manual skills. The change to the nature of work in developed nations, especially due to the production and adoption of increasingly sophisticated technologies, has also meant that the levels of education and training required in general have been elevated. Therefore, the educational goals for women at home who wish to re-enter the workforce are gradually increasing and becoming more difficult to achieve.

Open and distance education have provided educational choices for women who are based in the home with young children to help them pursue their aspirations and needs.[1] However, no open learning pack or distance education course minds the children, cleans the toilets and does the ironing; rather these educational incursions into the home add further demands which can be very difficult to reconcile with existing home activities. Hence, for women based at home, the choice of studying mainly from home is a mixed blessing, but one which is often worth the effort. Carol left school and went to teachers' college because she believed it was the best of the three options available to girls in the 1960s (the others being nursing and secretarial work). After some years primary teaching she married a farmer, resigned from her job and went to live on the farm. She had four children and found fitting into country life quite pleasant through the 1970s.

I had a wonderful time doing community work and going to the school and teaching drama as a volunteer. I was very busy with the children and the farm too. I enrolled in a course, off-campus (distance education) to train as a breast feeding counsellor. I got some very detailed essay questions to do, plus discussions at monthly meetings. I still found the time to do that. It was something I quite enjoyed. I was leading a group as well as doing the study at that stage because our group leader had left town. So that kept me very busy and that was really rewarding. The skills I picked up, the counselling skills, have been really helpful with my present job.

Carol's present job is as a neighbourhood (community) house coordinator. However, it was her pursuit of a previous job, together with the family's economic circumstances, which made her decide to study further.

We considered whether, with the small children and the ones at school, I could manage a job because farming was not really much of a return on investment at that stage, and we were really battling. The drought and poor farm prices were hitting us hard. I was on unemployment benefits because farmers' wives were able to get them then: it's changed now. I was managing on that, trying to run the household and feed and clothe the children. I was getting support from my family. My sister would send clothes and help out. I was forever running short of money and some weekends we would just live out of the garden, zucchinis, lettuce, carrots, tomatoes. Well I would make soup and we had salad and we had that with toast. So it seemed we would do better if I got a job. There were no teaching jobs in the local schools. However, there was a job in the local centre for adults with intellectual disabilities. I thought I'd be a certainty for the job. It was full-time but we thought we could manage. I knew the manager's secretary really well and – nudge, nudge, wink, wink – you will be alright! I didn't even get to the short list for the interview. I was told that there were five other applicants and they were all better qualified than me. I was stunned. It really came home to me that I was falling behind. I decided there and then to upgrade my qualifications.

Carol enrolled in a distance education course for the following year and then began the task of balancing home life and study. Towards the end of the year she obtained her job and then had the task of juggling all three during the next year.

I had a child at kindergarten, so I would go in four times a week with him and I would use the time he was at kinder and go around to the park and study. That was the idea, anyway. Really what I would do was look at the children playing on the swings, and watch the travellers who would come and all these people in their middle years bringing food with them, cakes and Thermoses and stuff. That fascinated me! I used to think 'I wonder what they have got to eat today?'. So I don't know when I did my study, but it was mainly in the daylight hours. If I could whizz through what I had to do around home and settle the pre-school child in front of Playschool on television or something, I would perhaps try to do a bit. I certainly don't remember studying at night like I have to force myself to do now. If only I had realized how difficult it would get the following year when I had a job as well.

As a trained primary school teacher, Carol had obtained an educational standard above most people and was also confident in her abilities to contribute to the voluntary educational, cultural and welfare activities of her community. It was her buffeting by the economic and meteorological climates of the early 1980s which pushed her to confront the labour market. She took action immediately to improve her qualifications. As a teacher she soon recognized the solution and didn't feel too perturbed by returning to study. June, however, chose study for quite different reasons. Whereas Carol would have happily enjoyed her life as 'farmer's wife' had it not been for the economic circumstances, June was feeling increasingly alienated at home in a rural community. She turned to studying at a distance to help her reconnect with society.

As a mother with young children I would spend time building bricks and playing in the sandpit with them. Then they started to go to school and I knew they were going to outgrow me. They'd go to college or university. I had this vision of me still playing in the sandpit. I knew I had to do something to remain in touch.

I think distance learning is a marvellous thing. I mean it really opened a door for me. I moved here two months before my eldest child was born and I didn't know a soul. I couldn't go out to work. I couldn't go out socializing with a baby. I was completely isolated really. I felt I was going up the wall before I started my course. It filled a lot of my life. It brought me into contact with ideas which normally I would have got through mixing with other people. I did it secondhand through lectures and the ideas you met on the course, and residential school, too, was marvellous. It was the first time I had been away on my own since I had left home and

I had been tied to the family ever since. One doesn't entirely leave a young family, but the sense of freedom was quite astonishing. It helped me stay with the human race, as it were, and I wouldn't have got a job without it. The job is helping, too, because I think a woman can be very, very isolated. I think you have got to keep your independence one way or another. If you are at home all the time you tend to be just a nobody, just a housewife, well a housewife with a BA is better than just a housewife!

June encapsulates how women can become 'prisoners of gender' if they follow what used to be considered the traditional path in early adulthood into marriage, a family and being a 'housewife'. Contemporary societies, in some respects, are more isolating for women at home than in the past. Not only is the domestic labour required in the home less dependent on regular, everyday work, but the more mobile and distributed nature of paid work often means that their breadwinning partners take the family far away from extended family contact in order to find work and build careers. It is true that modern communications and mass media technologies can provide for different forms of connections between people, but often these seem to pour the troubles of the world into the home, rather than alleviating a person's isolation.[2] June felt these sorts of difficulties deeply. However, Carol exemplifies a woman who followed a 'traditional' career path for women – 'primary teaching' – but in so doing obtained educational and other experiences which left her with what she saw as a fulfilled life, although traditionally located around the home and community.

Many women who were children before the Second Wave of feminism broke on their shores (roughly, before the 1970s) can recount how their parents rarely saw their education as important in comparison with their brothers' and this left them inheriting the circumstances that June described. Frances's case provides a different example. She was born in 1944.

I come from a very strange background for this day and age because my mother didn't believe in education for girls. She was very bright herself and had worked, but was obsessed with education for boys.

Mandie was born in 1957 and had a similar experience.

I just got sick of school. I wanted to go on further to university, but my parents – mainly my mother – didn't see any reason why I should and she was a big block. Instead of letting me study she would make me do different things. I had a sister 13 years younger than myself, she was very disruptive when you are trying to study, you couldn't leave your books and go look up something. She was just at that age where you have got to keep them out of the road to study and my mother didn't worry. She left school very early so she didn't understand that. She couldn't see you needed to be left alone to study. I really had nowhere apart from in my bedroom, but it wasn't light enough and it would get very cold, too. So I would spread my books out on the dining room table and then it would be 'Pack your books up it is tea time', just when I'd sat down to study. Often I'd get started and then she'd say 'Go and see what your sister is doing', or just get me to do little things around the house. She didn't think that Dad should waste the money on sending me through university.

For such women, the choices afforded through open and distance education are ones which they grasp in adulthood because they feel deeply about how they have been deprived in childhood or adolescence by their parents. Over the years they have carried on with their lives but not forgotten that they missed out on continuing their education to a level to which they aspired. They are not just choosing study for its own sake or for some specific increase in their knowledge and skills: they are choosing justice.

Gendered support and obstruction to study

For anyone to study successfully, it is usually important that the people closest to them in their lives support their endeavours in valuable ways. We have seen that in family circumstances some women, because of their sex, have received obstruction to their studying beyond the minimum years of schooling. However, there are those who received encouragement and support, both from their parents in terms of their educational goals and aspirations and also from their partners later in life. Stephanie was born in 1948 to a family with a relatively low income. Yet she recalls how her parents helped her through college.

I was the only one in the family, so I suppose that was a plus in my favour, if I had a brother or another sister or something it might not have been possible. Dad always believed it was important for girls to be educated as well and he couldn't see why girls shouldn't have the same education as boys in those days. Perhaps he was a forward thinker in that way. He and Mum encouraged me to stay at school and then paid for me to go to university because it was during the days when you had to pay fees. It was really difficult for them, but they really wanted me to go to university.

Stephanie became a school teacher and subsequently married and left teaching to have a family. She enrolled in further study at a distance to improve her qualifications with a view to returning to teaching.

> I had a lot of help from my husband. I don't think you can study unless your family supports you. He would help with the baby so I could get the assignments done.

In the gendered worlds of study, women are typically much more dependent than men on the support of their partners in order to complete their courses. Men are more likely to be involved in study as part of their work and may be receiving support in some form from their employers to complete their study. Women are more likely to be trying to balance a much heavier burden of study, work and home responsibilities. Generally, men find it easier to opt out of parenting responsibilities to study than do women. Therefore, it is women who most often express how good their partners are in supporting their study; men usually take such support for granted. David describes his wife's immediate agreement to his wishing to enrol in a course to pursue his own interests.

> She said, 'If you want to do it, you go ahead. Whatever it takes.' I mean all these books and study materials are not out on the table just because you were coming today. This is how it is unless I am told to get rid of it. Fifty weeks of the year this is how it is.

William, in his 60s, believed that his decision to study and the implications of this were quite acceptable to his wife. He told of a smooth domestic life which enabled him to study according to a regular schedule.

> I finish work in the evening, five o'clock, home, have a meal, put my feet up for ten minutes and then get cracking, until about ten o'clock. Weekday evenings, I try, if I am a bit behind then I will work on the weekend, but I try to leave the weekend alone actually.

> She is very tolerant, there is obviously lots of things I should be doing when I am doing this business, you can see things that need doing all the time, I have to put them off and then it is usually the winter then when you have this break and there is not a lot you can do then. She is very tolerant, you know.

Of course, William's views may not necessarily concur with those of his wife! Mandie's experience with her partner was confirmed by him, coincidentally, after our interview. Mandie, whose mother obstructed her attempts to study as a schoolgirl, had worked through a sequence of factory jobs and nightclasses to enrol in a degree course at a distance. At the time we spoke she was living with her boyfriend and they were expecting their first child, although Mandie already had a child from a previous relationship.

> A lot of thought and talking to my boyfriend had gone into me taking up study. We realized that I wouldn't be able to do everything. It would be on him to pay for certain things. We had worked it all out that I couldn't work, do the course and have time for my daughter as well. Something had to give and it had to be work. He realized that and he was quite happy to help with housework because there were days when it was getting close to when assignments were due and he would have to do the chores or the meals each night.

> My boyfriend suggested we get a computer to help with my assignments. It made it a lot easier and gave better presentation. We would print out a rough copy, go through it, read it out loud, work out what wasn't right. It probably took a lot longer, every weekend for six months sitting on the computer, feeding information in, printing out and then fixing it up. One thing I wouldn't have been able to do without is my boyfriend as a proof reader. I think he is very intelligent. He would just proof read all my stuff, he would miss a few little bits, and I picked them up later. He would make suggestions and I would get so wild, saying 'What was wrong with that?'. To start with it was very hard, to accept being criticized for what I had written. It would take hours to do and he would criticize different sections of it, but then when you sat there and read it out loud and thought about it, it didn't even flow, it didn't even sound logical.

Mary shows another example of the ways in which the men in women's lives help or hinder their studies. Mary, in her late 50s, is a secretary and her husband is a draughtsperson. She shows how fragile a woman's confidence can be in her abilities to study and how selfish and unhelpful a man can be.

> In 1980 my boss suggested that I do a degree part-time. Before that my husband had been talking about doing one himself, although he had architectural qualifications he didn't have a degree. So we both decided to apply simultaneously. I don't know whether he thought I was capable of doing it to be honest. Probably quite right. My boss suggested it as a good

idea, so I thought, 'Yes what a jolly good idea, maybe I will do that'.

I was terrified. In no way did I think I would be able to do university work. Especially when looking back, as a child you think of university and hold it very much in awe. I don't think I ever thought I could ever reach university. As my boss had suggested it, I was very determined to give it a good go. I was not going to let him think I am chickening out before I tried. So I thought I would give it a go the first year and see how I got on. Petrified the whole year. I had a dreadful year because I was such a nervous person during that year. I used to hate going to tutorials. I never thought I was good enough, suffered from a bit of an inferiority complex really. I don't know why I should have done because there is no reason why I should be any worse than the others, we were all very much the same age, funnily enough.

I was dreading my first assignment. I thought all I wanted was a pass. The first grade I got was a credit. I was jumping up and down with glee. I mean a credit is very ordinary, we know that now, but in those days to have got a credit with my first essay was tremendous. The fact that I had done it at all, I could have had a failure, couldn't I? If I did fail I would not have gone on because, even though I was determined, I also couldn't have coped with rejection. That was very much in my home background, you weren't allowed to reveal your own thoughts and things, it is probably partly my own fault because I should have insisted, shouldn't I? It is partly to do with the background and how you are yourself. I was fairly docile in those days, what my mother and father said was the Word.

Then there was residential school. I had to organize everything. My husband didn't think about that side of things. That was my job. I always think with women when they have a family, they have to split themselves up into so many little parcels. When you study it means you have to split yourself even more. I always think that it tends to be a bit unfair, it is certainly not the same these days, I know, but I think it is unfair. I have always had to do this when I have been doing it over the years. I have had to put the house right, do the shopping, get everything in. Get all these things organized for the residential school – like ask my mother to come up to look after the children. Then after everything else is done, I may have time to think about myself and do a bit of study. My husband is not a great believer in helping around the house – so perhaps I was unlucky there – he may wipe a few dishes, but that's about it. It was never a case of 'Look we are both doing study, therefore we shall split the duties', it was always 'You have got to get this done and then you will have a bit of time for yourself'. One advantage I had was the fact that my boss isn't here at work every day and so he encouraged me to do study here if I had nothing else to do. He also lets me take leave for residential school. He's very supporting, not like my husband.

An irony of Mary's story is that the closest man in her life hindered her studies and yet 'her boss', another man, originated her consideration of enrolling and then encouraged and supported her thereafter. Mary's self-esteem was low, something which is common with adult students returning to study after a long absence. Mary shows that new students should consider that, if so many people have gone before them, there is no good reason why *they* should not succeed. Mary believed that she had been 'unlucky' in the fact that her husband did not take his share of the responsibilities in the home and that 'it was certainly not the same these days'. Carol, however, shows that this is not necessarily the case. Carol is from the next generation to Mary and, although she experienced many of the same pressures, she was able to stake a claim for herself to have time to study. She recounts the story of a weekend when her husband suggested that she reconsider her priorities.

It is very difficult. My job is supposed to be 20 hours a week, but it is more than that. So I count up the hours that I work overtime and then during school holidays and crisis time I can have a couple of days off. But it has been difficult with the family because they have had illnesses and things through the year. There are also crisis times for my husband who is very busy and works long hours too. So we are two parents working fairly long hours so, I am afraid, I use my weekends and I don't work on a Monday. So I have what I call my long weekend and that is basically study. I try to do it at night, but then there are meetings and other things.

There is a bit of family pressure at the moment to say, 'Look, Mum, we have had enough of all this studying'. My husband said the other weekend – poor man – 'I think it is about time you considered giving up study.' I said, 'Why?' and he said, 'Because the children are getting to the stage in their schooling where they will need more of your time.' I said, 'In what way? Do you mean that I will need to spend some time with them with their homework?'. He said, 'Not so much that, but just keeping the place running smoothly so that they are not hassled because you have got to find time to study.' I replied 'And what are you going to do? What are you going to give up to contribute towards your children's schooling?' He said that he wished he hadn't opened his mouth and that he was digging a deeper and deeper hole for himself. I am getting the vibes, 'What will you have at the end of this? Will it enhance you job opportunities?' and all that sort of thing.

I know I gave him a fairly hard time that weekend when I had done quite a bit of research. I didn't realize how much I had done, and then I had to collate all this and I had a deadline for an assignment. I usually like to be well-organized and get them all done well ahead, but it was real pressure. I was getting up at 5.30 so I could be at the computer by 6.00. I was still taking the children and their bikes to the river to play. I was fitting in the family things, working really early in the morning and then the other end of the day, so the pressure was on and perhaps I gave him a hard time over that one.

Claire is of a similar age to Carol – some 25 years younger than Mary. Claire experienced many of the same difficulties, but her husband was not inclined to reconsider the gender relations which provided him with a mother and then a wife (and mother-in-law) to minister to his domestic needs and assume some of his parenting responsibilities. Claire is a highly qualified nurse and is in charge of a form of specialist theatre nursing in a large teaching hospital. She is married to a physician at the hospital and they have three young children.

Men, like my husband, have been brought up by mothers who stay at home and look after the house. The men go to work and earn money and that is how they have their meat and two veg on Sunday. That is how they have all been brought up – they are changing slowly, but it is a hell of a fight to get them to change. He is thoroughly down on me studying now and will do nothing to help. The first time I had residential school I organized everything and then left him with the two kids. I mean all the childcare was in place, as usual, I organized meals, but it was all too much for him.

The first residential school was freedom. For the first time in my life I could really be a student! I realized what I had missed out on not going to university. The lecturers had a totally different approach than I was used to with my nurse training. The work was hard, but if you went to lectures or whatever that was up to you and if you didn't, that was your loss. Consequently everybody went to everything, which was really refreshing after being told in nurse training that you must be in the classroom at 9 o'clock and to be generally treated like children. The social side of residential school was good and the teaching side of it was brilliant.

The next residential school I was eight and half months pregnant, so I had to miss it. This year it is not too far away from home. But it doesn't make any difference because I have still got to organize a household and three children before I can go. The children will still be going to childminding which they go to when I am at work. My mother is coming down to live here for a week because my husband says he can't manage to get all three kids up, dressed, to the childminder and get himself to work on time. I do so everyday, but he can't for one week! So my mother will look after him and the house, and the children. And the dogs have had to go to kennels. He says that everything in the house, including the dogs, is my responsibility.

Probably part of me studying is a kind of rebellion against all the domestic things being my responsibility. Other women talk about these problems all the time to each other, at residential school, married women anyway. I haven't met anyone that hasn't got the same sorts of problems that I have, it is not that husbands don't try, they do try, but they have been brought up in a way that they have no conception of the work involved in a household and family, no idea at all. He is now not prepared to do any more to help me study. He thinks that he has got enough on his plate without doing extra for me to study. So I am studying under the condition that it doesn't intrude too much and if I get desperate – to write an essay or do something – he will, if I ask, take all the kids out for a couple of hours, but two hours here and there isn't an awful lot of help.

Claire's husband behaved during the interview in a way which was consistent with her remarks. He interrupted the interview to pursue domestic matters and then made comments after the interview about the amount of study his wife did and how 'it was difficult for her'! It is hard to underestimate the immense difficulties some women will face with their partners. Many of these women will find themselves in an untenable position such that if they 'stake their claim' in the home and family, personal and family relations might become so difficult that they either give in or leave. Men, like William, who claim that their partners are very cooperative when they wish to take up study, are often using traditional gender relations to take whatever they want out of the home and family resources. Men who are contemplating study should ask themselves if they are like Mary and Claire's partners and proposing to exploit their partners still further.

Changing times?

The women's stories show that the worlds of learning for men and women are usually markedly different. It is relatively unusual to find a woman learner like Mandie who has a partner who contributes a lot to her study. It is much more usual to find men learners who assume their partner's support and then take it for granted throughout their courses. The women who have significant partners' support do not take it for granted; they are often extremely grateful, even though for the most part, these supportive men are often doing little more than could reasonably be expected in a fair, egalitarian world. These contrasts are a product of the gendered social worlds in which studying takes place and with which it intersects. They are not things that open and distance educators can ignore if they wish to do their jobs properly.[3]

Some women are studying, in part, as a personal and political statement in relation to their past and present injustices. They are staking a claim both about, and for, themselves. Sometimes men are also making statements of a similar kind in relation to their previous backgrounds, often in terms of proving themselves as being able to complete a course, obtain a degree, etc.

Some men and women reach a new realization of themselves through their courses and reject aspects of their pasts which they learn to disdain. A student told me after an interview we had just recorded that before she began studying, she used to get very frustrated and short-tempered, at home all day with her toddler. On one occasion, after a particularly protracted piece of annoying behaviour while she was cleaning upstairs, she pushed her child away and the child fell down a flight of stairs. The shock was enormous for her because, although the child only suffered minor bruising, she was terrified to admit what happened for fear of being accused of doing it deliberately (I understood that this was the first time she had revealed it). She believed that over the years, her studies had helped her cope with such pressures, partly by understanding the nature of them more and partly by being, like June at the beginning of this chapter, connected through her study to what she saw as a more meaningful and fulfilling world outside.

George provides another powerful example of changes through learning from the other side of the gender divide. His background story of a difficult schooling and a terrifying basic training during National Service is told in Chapter 2.

I feel that since I started and I have been studying it has broadened my outlook in certain ways. I have met other people – although I am rather reticent about pushing myself forward. I have met other people and I have met some nice people. I would like to get on and do a bit more because I find that as I learn more about myself and things I don't get frustrated, irritable and angry. My wife has put up with me for the last 30 years. I have a very bad temper and I am ashamed to say so, but I have taken it out on her. Since I have been doing the course I have been more settled. I have been able to adjust myself, control myself and look at things differently. Rather than having a Bolshi attitude. That is what I like about it, it has helped me to adjust myself.

George was admitting that he no longer beat his wife – an act which epitomizes the abuse of women and the degradation of men. It is possible to see men and women changing themselves through their studies and trying to create new futures – in effect, they can be portrayed as becoming more 'open' people as they become more 'open' learners. The parts that open and distance education play within this have been very significant, although it would be incorrect to assume that this has been a deliberate intention of the institutions, although it would be so for some courses, perhaps. The impression is that the students themselves make their courses into what they want of them for themselves. Some grab an opportunity to study because their parents denied them such. Some want to connect with the 'real' world outside of their homes. Some want to obtain a qualification to obtain a job. Some want to enhance their qualifications to re-enter the workforce after childrearing.

A question for prospective or new students could well be, 'Do they realize the potentially far-reaching implications of studying?' A question for open and distance educators could well be, 'If these personal transformations occur without them intending it, can they claim to be offering an education which addresses the needs of women (or of gender equity more broadly)?' Or is this just an unintended consequence?

Notes

1 Margaret Grace and I have discussed the ways in which the education of women has been 'privatized' through distance education, in the sense that distance education pushes women's education into their private worlds rather than bringing them into the public spheres of education and training facilities. See, Evans, T D and Grace, M (1994) 'Distance education and the gendered privatisation of learning', *Journal of*

Curriculum Studies (in press). Jackie Cook presents an argument about the advantages of women's distance education being removed from what, in effect, are the masculine worlds of education and training. She found that teaching a course for Australian women while she was on leave in China provided some unanticipated benefits due to the 'liberation' from her institution. See, Cook, J (1989), 'The liberation of distance: teaching Women's Studies from China', in Evans, T D and Nation, D E (eds) *Critical Reflections on Distance Education*, London: Falmer Press, pp. 23–37.

2 Judy Wacjman has explored several aspects of technology from a feminist perspective. She questions the masculine assumptions behind the development of many technologies. Given that educational technologies are deeply embedded in broader technological shifts, Wacjman's critique has considerable relevance to the open and distance educator or trainer. See, Wacjman, J (1991) *Feminism Confronts Technology*, Cambridge: Polity Press/Sydney: Allen & Unwin.

3 Those who would like to take these matters further could begin with Faith, K (ed.) (1989) *Toward New Horizons for Women in Distance Education: International perspectives*, London: Routledge. For a detailed review of the literature and issues in the field see, Grace, M (1991) 'Gender issues in distance education', in Evans, T D and King, B (eds) *Beyond the Text: Contemporary writing on distance education*, Geelong: Deakin University Press, pp. 56–74.

Chapter 5

Power: encounters with those in control

Power and control in open and distance education

A significant part of our school experiences as children is taken up with matters of discipline and control. 'Kid's culture' seems to have always involved a concern for resisting teachers' authority, escaping their clutches or, occasionally 'getting one back' over them. From the earliest school novels through to the television series of today, these sorts of experiences and meanings are portrayed, replayed and, importantly, reconstructed for the next generation of 'school kids'. On leaving school, things do not always get better. As George told of his post-school experiences in Chapter 2: night school was avoided by apprentices wherever possible and basic training during National Service certainly lived up to its name. Likewise, in the same chapter Michael's loss of interest in his night classes on insurance was noted and, in Chapter 4, Claire contrasted her glimpse of 'real' university education with the authoritarian nature of her nursing training.

For many learners in open and distance education, their schooling and, sometimes, their post-school experiences as adults, reflect models of education which are not consistent with the independent learning required for their open and distance study. However, this independent learning is not of the unfettered, unstructured and unscheduled kind. Rather, it is an independence within the limits of the assessment schedules and prescriptions, within the timetabled activities or events and, perhaps most importantly, within the pedagogical and curricular parameters of the course materials, and the tutors or assessors who mediate them. It seems that for most students, the independence of open and distance education is a liberation of a kind which they accept and a few even cherish. They have the power to study at a place and time of their choosing; this power, more than anything else, probably explains distance education's popularity with adult learners.

Adults' engagements with open and distance education are, however, often founded on highly didactic models[1] – such as those of instructional design – which provide them with little control over their own learning. Typically, in any teaching relationship the balance of power, authority and control is usually seen to be tipped in favour of the teacher rather than the learner. The teacher is often seen as the 'expert' or the repository of the desired knowledge and skills, and the learner needs to 'keep in' with the teacher to survive and succeed. Amy, who is in her 70s, makes the following point:

> You have to stick with what they say in the unit and learn what sort of a bod your tutor is, get on the right wavelength and you are all right. Does that sound nice and cynical? It is so.

Amy's point was made in relation to her experience of tutors on her open education course. However, it is the sort of point which is often made about teachers with whom students interact. Such a point is a lot more difficult to make in relation to assessment which is carried out by computer or other non-human means but, even then, there remains an element of students trying to understand what the teacher 'behind' the computer really wants.[2]

In forms of open and distance education where substantial course materials 'carry' the teaching, then one might argue that the authority of the teacher is substantially irrelevant, except at the point of assessment or tutoring. However, the authority of the teachers is actually solidified in the printed and other texts in a way which can, in effect, render them less challengeable than if they were face-to-face with their students, for example. The curriculum is usually crafted into highly produced forms which are mediated through print, audio and/or video. Unless the teacher has relinquished some authority – perhaps by deliberately debating the problematic nature of what they are teaching and how it is being taught – and created 'space' for the students to shape their own learning, then the students are left with little option but to adhere to the curriculum (which is often some years old) and its required learning styles.[3]

Damien's story reflects the case of a student who finds that both the curriculum and the teaching were not to his liking.

I did two journalism courses. I got thoroughly disgusted with the people teaching it, and the way they were marking it. I had spent four years as a photo journalist and I knew some of the things they were teaching and I got a bit disgusted with them.

When I did the second journalism course I found that I had to take my holidays half way through the course, I was going overseas. Unfortunately, what the staff don't recognize is that people have holidays and they don't coincide with education institution's holidays. I got the course guide and checked through it for the assignments and due dates. I phoned to confirm those dates, because I had been told at work that I had to take so many holidays within a particular time. I was told that those dates were right. Fine, then the course package arrives and it changes the dates and we effectively lost two weeks study time. As I had to take three weeks holidays as well, it meant I was having to complete the course in five weeks less time than normal.

I phoned up the journalism people and they said 'Those dates are right'. I told them about my study and holidays, but it is just typical of that department, all the people teaching that course. They didn't care and weren't going to let me have any more time. I have heard some people say, 'Oh well that's journos'. That is the way they act. I can't recommend the course to anybody.

I have done other courses and if you have got a problem you ring your tutor and they will be really helpful. With the first journalism course I phoned them up five times and I never got a reply and the tutors never phoned me back once. The administrative staff phoned back and told me that they had passed my message on. On another occasion I phoned up and asked for somebody to phone me regarding a particular question and nobody did. You can just phone them and phone them.

Damien was very bitter about his experiences on the journalism courses. As he notes, his experiences contrasted with others where tutors were prompt and helpful with their comments. His frustrations were exacerbated by his inability to communicate his feelings when phone calls were not returned, and when he was able to make contact, by the apparent unwillingness of the tutor to make any allowances for his problems. There are often staff on profession-related courses who are reluctant to adopt more open approaches to their teaching. They see this as diluting professional standards if people are able to complete the course without all the 'disciplines' of the profession. One can imagine that journalists teaching a course would argue that deadlines were very much a part of the profession and students who could not keep to them on their courses should not be accommodated.

Damien's frustrations with studying at a distance also extended to another course he undertook, this time in the area of religious studies.

> I also did a religion course which I thought was the biggest no-hope thing ever. Some of the comments I got back from the people were such things as they wanted me to resit the paper, which I refused to do and yet they still passed me, I told them they could fly a kite. I was told that I wasn't sympathetic with the views of the course and that the people I quoted in my assignments weren't credible. I don't see how you can claim that the authority I was using isn't a credible source – he is a lecturer at another university – so I refused to submit the paper, but I still got a pass. I thought it was a waste of time subject and I would never advise anybody to do it.

Clearly, Damien did not agree with the 'views of the course'. In areas such as religion, which have been the scene of wars, intimidation and dispute, it is unsurprising that in the study of them, there are academic disputes of some magnitude. What should the teachers' position be in instances where the student works against the implicit or explicit philosophy of the course? How should an open educator, in particular, react? How does the power differential between teacher and student come in to play? These are difficult questions to answer when the course is embedded in deep values of, for example, a religious kind. It raises questions for students concerning whether their approach should be to 'toe the line', as Amy explained previously, or to assert their own viewpoint.

Damien's difficulties were principally concerning power and control between student and teachers, a matter that is pursued further in the next section; more broadly, students are located *en masse* in a relatively powerless position within their institutions. This is related to the 'distances' between the students and their open and distance education institutions, and between the students themselves. On campus, students can more easily share their gripes and grievances, and even take forms of collective action which can vent their frustrations and may lead to favourable changes. Part-time students, often studying separately from one another and at a distance from the centre of their institutions, have to rely on forms of mediated communication to deal with their problems. If letters, phone calls, faxes or email are not replied to, then they remain relatively powerless to do anything about it.

This is not all. Institutions of open and distance education impose their own bureaucratic control over their students (and teachers!). Some of these institutions are enormous, with hundreds of thousands of students distributed over entire nations and beyond. At the other extreme are small 'boutique' organizations which may have a few hundred students and staff; they may even be small departments of larger industrial, professional or service organizations. The relative power that students have in these organizations is probably related to organizational size, but obviously factors such as organizational structure and culture, formal and informal student representation and the organizations' receptiveness to the needs of learners, play a part. The learners' own personal predispositions and their power and influence also affect the ways in which they contest both their teachers and their organizations.

Confronting teachers

Pat was in her late 50s and had been trained in singing and music. She was pursuing a degree and had encountered a course in language and literacy which jarred with her previous learning.

> I just found that was more important to me than merely speaking just to a tutor – don't get me wrong – there have been some very good tutors, which I loved, really and truly some were very helpful. But in certain subjects that I have undertaken, it was very difficult. More so with some of my background and with the studies that I have done. In one particular subject we were talking about phonetics in the tutorial. Now I have been trained in phonetics with speech therapy. I found we [Pat and the tutor] became at cross purposes, very much so. I look at the logic and the scientific way of phonetics. I couldn't help but put that point forward because that is the way to put it!

Pat was using the opportunity of her tutorials to resist the understanding of phonetics which the course materials and the tutor were expounding. With her experience and previous study she felt confident enough to put her viewpoint, but not to press the matter further, even though she thought that, at least, there was another legitimate ('logical' and 'scientific') viewpoint and, one formed the impression, that maybe she thought the content of the course on the matter of phonetics was wrong. Assuming a student was absolutely correct and their course was wrong, how could a student, such as Pat, go about changing the course? What sort of processes would be involved? How much effort would it take to be successful? Later in this chapter Frances's contest with her institution (not so much over a matter of curriculum as teaching) will be explored in more detail. It shows just how difficult it can be to change things or protest about inadequacies.

Amy's experience was that she was quite happy to study her course, but found some of the tutorial and residential school encounters she was required to experience reflected ideological positions to which she was opposed. She found that many tutors forced their opinions on students and were dogmatic. She felt she was unable to discuss things with them.

> The residential school was ridiculous, even the lecturers were all carrying banners. I am not against it because it was left-wing. It was not just that. It was left- and right-wing, from fascist to communist. They were all there, seeing things from one angle. Have you tried to reason with such people? Have you ever tried talking to people who are convinced they are right? I am one of them about certain things! It was not worth bothering with. I used to expect them to produce collapsible soap-boxes and start spouting away.

Amy's experiences were undoubtedly framed by her own ideological views which seemed to be at variance with the 'banner-carrying' tutors. Whatever the circumstances actually were (and other students I interviewed who had taken the same course on this and other years made similar, if less graphic, comments), there is certainly the case that Amy felt unable to interact with her teachers on at least these aspects of her learning. She felt powerless to counter the teachers' control over the knowledge and values which were being conveyed.

Confronting institutions

Confronting individual teachers in an education or training situation takes a significant degree of assertion and an understanding of one's power. Pat did challenge her tutors, whereas Amy decided against it, although in Chapter 8 Amy recounts an occasion when she *did* counter some of her fellow students in the defence of another student (see p 116). Pat's problems with her institution had extended to the bureaucratic. She believed that when she originally enrolled, she had been misinformed about the course she should follow. She wanted to obtain a teaching qualification, but had been directed to an Arts course as the most appropriate way for her to obtain her qualification. After completing some courses she decided to ask how her studies would lead her to her intended goal.

I would like to get in on the education side though and this is where I think I was mis-advised initially when I went out there. I should have been more specific. Well, I didn't really know what to ask. It was another new world to me. Trying to find out about the right course. They didn't spell out the type of subjects that were available and what would be suitable for me.

Now I have only switched over to education this year. I have done philosophy, I have got a minor in philosophy if you like, and I have done social studies, literature and performing arts, and what else. Really and truly that to me is not getting me towards the goal that I want to get to because I want to teach music. You see, I should have been redirected into education.

Then I was told that possibly they wouldn't accept me into education because I wasn't going out into schools, being a teacher in a school classroom. But I am teaching here all the time. I am not just teaching primary school kids. I am very concerned at the fact that, from the speech therapy viewpoint and from the music viewpoint, a lot of the newly qualified teachers are going out into the field with only two or three sessions on how to correct these problems with children. And here is me, a specialist in that particular field, and they are not quite interested! I can't see the logic of that. Anyway I have spoken to the course adviser in education. It must have been the fighting spirit the day I spoke to him! He told me to go over towards the end of the year and see them.

Pat was hopeful that her case would be heard sympathetically and that she could transfer to the teacher education course and obtain a teaching qualification. It is difficult to tell whether the original course adviser was entirely at fault in giving her advice about the subjects she should study, or whether Pat's unfamiliarity with the culture of the institution led her to be both reticent and also imprecise in her questions and needs. If the student is relatively powerless, then arguably, the potential student is even more so, certainly in terms of knowing how to penetrate the bureaucracy and have one's claims recognized. Students, especially ones who have been studying for some time, even at a distance, usually have some understanding of their institution through the various communications and experiences they have. They also often have student organizations to provide information and represent their cases if need be.[4] Potential students have to rely on personal knowledge, strategies and skills to ensure that they obtain the best information they can and take the best decision on their course as a consequence.

Frances's story is worth pursuing at some length here because it essentially deals with the institutional bureaucracy, although the origin of her (and others') problems rested in the teaching situation. She enrolled in her course as a 'bright-eyed and bushy-tailed' learner who was vitally interested in learning for its own sake.

> I thought it would be just fun. I have got so many things I have done like that. So when I went to the Arts course I found it quite fun. It was nothing more or less than that. I was interested in reading the material and then reading around as much as I could. I was disappointed to find that, not only did they not encourage you to read more widely, but they actively discouraged it. That worried me. And it still worries me because I am doing a social science course this year. I thought it would be very different, broad-minded about these things, but they are just the same.

> I have worked this out, I think I know why. I think that all open entry distance learning, when it is taking people in with no formal qualifications, has to cope with a very widely disparate group. Some people come with a degree and want to do a different degree. Others come in with no formal qualifications at all, say age 50, having not written an essay at all. They could have gone right through their lives and never structured an essay. Or you could have people coming in with A levels. I think they want to bring it all down to one simple kind of unit. So what they do does not actually allow for anybody to extend too far one way or the other because that will complicate the marking system, it will complicate the tutorials, because people will be throwing in ideas which a lot of people won't be able to grapple with. It does worry me because the course is one where, because of my interest in politics, I would like to spend a lot more time reading to some purpose that I could use in my essays. I did actually try it, but it was not appreciated at all. I still read.

Frances felt powerless to manage her own learning, but had rationalized the circumstances in a way which helped her accommodate the difficulties. She was, in fact, saying that her lack of control over her own learning was a feature of the form of open learning at a distance in which she was engaged. As her course unfolded, she found that more difficulties were in her way. She said she, and some other students, were now infamous.

Infamous! Let us be honest. In the literature course I came to grief with the tutor. It is a course which is based on a group of novels and I thought the idea of it was that one was going to examine critical theories of English literature and European literature. It is something that intrigues me enormously and on one occasion I asked our tutor if she would devote one of her tutorials to structuralism, which is in the course material. She not only refused, but also said she didn't believe in it and certainly didn't know very much about it. I was rattled because I had been going along to these tutorials and they really were awfully boring. They were lectures really and then she would ask us to read chunks of material.

On top of this she'd turn up half an hour late. OK, anybody can do so if they stay half an hour afterwards, but she also went 20 minutes early! She was always so bad-tempered and really very anti-student as far as one could see. I mean everything she did, it was quite ridiculous. She gave you marks if you actually put the title of your essay at the top of the page! Great ticks all over the place. The thing that really bugged me and another girl was that we tried to get some stimulating discussions going during the tutorials and the tutor would say, 'Would you mind not talking about that because I don't think anybody else understands.' Anybody who raised anything which one might call vaguely outside the text in front and the storyline was just squashed. It struck me, for a university course, as being just a bit off to be honest. In the end there were about seven of us who were having tremendous difficulties with this woman.

I was about to write to the institution – and I am not a complaining sort of person – to say 'Watch out because this woman is going to teach this course next year and she is not helping anybody'. I was concerned because that year I studied a history course which really did something for me. Why shouldn't other students have the same opportunity to be taught by people who really do set their minds alight? That is what learning is all about. You are disadvantaged enough studying at a distance, but to have, on top of all that, a tutor like we had on the literature course who was completely against any original thought at all, really annoyed me. She marked our essays and she was putting us down, and I mean putting us down, really belittling us. It is unforgivable to belittle anyone. It is quite difficult to belittle women of my age and get away with it, and she really was belittling these women. One of them is a JP locally and the poor thing had failed this course the previous year with this tutor and was taking it a second time. She wasn't getting any help at all. I really was very upset, and so we got together and wrote a letter to the institution.

I insisted that the letter should be copied to central administration as well as to the person in charge of the study centre which employs her. It was dealt with by the head of the counselling service. I can show you the letters. He was saying, 'What right have you to complain? We have been very satisfied with this woman over the years. We have had very satisfactory reports of her. We can't see that there is any substance in your complaints. Please itemize your complaints with dates'. Well, could you itemize a list of complaints over a year, actually note the times and exact things that had happened?

It is very difficult, but it struck me as an extraordinary way to approach the whole thing. They are fundamentally saying, 'You are not a person equal to me. You are some kind of sub-being who I can put down'. I wasn't prepared to take this because, I thought, damn it all, why should we? So we got together and we wrote another letter, a much more detailed letter, each of us itemizing our complaints. After a very long period of time we had a letter back and the only person they apologized to was me. It wasn't really an apology, but they actually admitted that I was right to complain about the structuralism thing. I actually got an admission that she should have been able to deal with it. You can tell the extent to which any notice was taken of our points because this year the tutor was given an extra course to teach. A fourth level (even higher level) course! The others were so sickened.

We were also frightened because we were told that our complaints would remain confidential. But this year we were made aware of the fact that we were troublemakers. The person who is teaching this year is delightful and she is very good at what she does, but she spent ten minutes at the beginning of the first session this year saying how complaints procedures were dealt with, etc. I had never had that happen in my life before, it was self-evidently because I was there in the group.

Frances's story is one which will not surprise experienced educators. Occasionally these sorts of problems occur and they are very difficult to deal with because so much of the teaching relationship (especially of a face-to-face kind) rests on good faith. It also rests on the unpredictability of interpersonal relations in group settings. It is impossible to know exactly what was involved in the tutorial events which Frances describes. Frances portrays herself as almost the ideal independent adult learner: keen, enquiring, reading, thinking, motivated. Her explanation of her initial experience of being discouraged from reading beyond the course materials (and this was an observation other students had made) displayed an understanding of institutional, educational and individual problems and concerns.[5] Her experiences with the tutor are also ones which could be substantiated by other students (and she did offer to provide the names of the other students involved) and, of course, there were the letters and documents sent and received. Clearly, these learners had an experience which was not of the kind that they expected as adult students. In some respects their learning experiences seemed shaped by a tutor who used some of the more negative features of school education and, in contrast to teaching children, the adults involved would not be 'belittled' by authoritarian, didactic approaches.

The institution's way of dealing with the complaints was, again, not surprising for the person who has been involved in educational (or other) institutions for any length of time. There are a variety of defence mechanisms which come into play, not necessarily to defend the person who is the object of the complaint, although that is often the case, but rather to defend the institution itself. In order to deal with these sorts of problems more constructively from the learner's perspective, the students do need to know that their complaints are being taken seriously. They see themselves as powerless and even 'frightened' in the face of the massed ranks of the organization which they feel has wronged them. In distance education – as was noted at the beginning of this chapter – the remoteness of students from the organization's bureaucratic heart contributes to this powerlessness. In open education, one might hope that the whole organization was open to student needs and concerns to the extent that the sort of experiences Frances and her colleagues experienced would never be so prolonged.[6]

What can students do in such circumstances, especially if their employer is also overseeing their 'open learning'? It is important to recognize that their complaints are likely to be dealt with bureaucratically. Therefore, documentation is all-important: thus keeping notes and records of events (or the lack of them) is often crucial. The friendly approach is often best at first. Perhaps the staff member who has been causing difficulty is actually under considerable stress themselves, maybe a family or work crisis is involved. If the difficulties are not resolved, then consulting student organizations, student counsellors, staff development officers, etc. may help. Sometimes they can act as advocates and resolve the problem without any formal representations. A further step is to write formally to the person concerned (and maybe send an official copy to their supervisor and/or the student organization). A final step is often to lodge a written complaint to the most senior person in the organization. Strategically, it is worth considering that total victories are few, Pyrrhic victories are usually pointless, and compromises are the hallmarks of democracy!

In this chapter the focus has been on students' stories of encounters which reflect their relative powerlessness in their learning situations. For most learners, these power relationships are implicit and lay dormant in their learning experiences. Certainly, there are explicit manifestations of the power which have been expressed in this and other chapters. The authority over what is learned, during what periods, in what contexts and how it will be assessed are, amongst other things, explicit manifestations. Forms of open education, and some forms of distance education, do relinquish some of these powers, and provide more authority to the learner to shape and control their own learning. Some might argue, however, that such relinquishment is only good for as long as the institutions involved sustain their intentions in this regard, and that they retain the power and authority to rescind. As a final question, one might query whether there can ever be other than (heavily?) circumscribed independent learning within an educational institution?[7]

Notes

1 Börje Holmberg has used the term 'guided didactic conversation' to advocate an approach to teaching at a distance that is actually somewhat oppositional to didacticism, which is concerned with 'instructing' or 'lecturing' people. I feel that, in English, Holmberg's approach is probably rather a 'guided educational conversation' or 'guided tutorial conversation'. See, Holmberg, B (1989) *Theory and Practice of Distance Education*, London: Routledge, pp. 43–6 for an account of his approach. See also, Gillard, G (1981)'The implied student-teacher dialogue in distance education', in Crump, P and Livingston, K (eds) *Australian and South Pacific External Studies Association Forum '81*, Suva: ASPESA; Juler, P (1990) 'Promoting interaction: maintaining independence: swallowing the mixture', *Open Learning* 5, 2, 24–33; Nation, D E (1991) 'Teaching texts and independent learning', in Evans, T D and King, B (eds) *Beyond the Text: Contemporary writing on distance education*, Geelong: Deakin University Press, pp. 101–129.

2 There appears to be scope for further research, theory and analysis on this matter. Philip Juler and Diana Laurillard have considered such matters (Juler, P A (1994) 'Do you read me?', in Parer, M (ed.) *Unlocking Open*

Learning, Churchill: Centre for Distance Learning, Monash University (in press); Laurillard, D (1988)) 'Computers and the emancipation of students: giving control to the learner', in Ramsden, P (ed.) *Improving Learning: New perspectives*, London: Kogan Page, pp. 215–23. In addition, the work collected by Robyn Mason and Tony Kaye has been significant; see, Mason, R and Kaye, A (eds) (1989) *Mindweave: Communication, computers and distance education*, Oxford: Pergamon.

3   These are difficult matters to resolve for educators who use highly mediated approaches. Daryl Nation has grappled with these issues in his teaching and has written about them (see, for example, Nation, D E (1987) 'Some reflections upon teaching sociology at a distance', *Distance Education*, 8, 2, 190–207, and Nation, D E (1991) in note 1). See also the following chapters from Evans, T D and Nation, D E (eds) (1989) *Critical Reflections on Distance Education*, London: Falmer Press: Cook, J, 'Teaching Women's Studies from China' (pp. 23–37); Fitzclarence, L and Kemmis, S A, 'Distance education curriculum for curriculum theory' (pp. 147–77); Modra, H, 'Using journals to encourage critical thinking at a distance' (pp. 123–46); Smyth, J, 'When teachers theorize their practice: a reflexive approach to a distance education course', (pp. 197–233). And from Evans, T D and Nation, D E (eds) (1993) *Reforming Open and Distance Education*, London: Kogan Page: Evans, T D, King, B and Nunan, T, 'Teaching towards critical research, reflection and practice in distance education' (pp. 36–54); Harris, D, 'Distance education at the margins' (pp. 55–71)). I have also discussed critically the implications of print-based curricula and pedagogies, in Evans, T D (1989) 'Fiddling while the tome turns: reflections of a distance education development consultant', in Parer, M (ed.) *Development, Design and Distance Education*, Churchill: Centre For Distance Learning, Gippsland Institute, pp. 117–26.

4   Margaret Grace has written of her experiences as an advocate for distance students. Her account shows that the power of both students' representatives and the students is heavily circumscribed by the social structures (including gender) of large educational institutions. She also shows that there is a real power to collective human agency. See, Grace, M (1989) '"Is the university awful?": political activism and consciousness raising among external students', in Evans, T D and Nation, D E (1989) *Critical Reflections on Distance Education*, London: Falmer Press, pp. 55–71. For a critical account of first year students' experiences of studying at a distance see, Grace, M (1992) 'Communication and meaning: the first year experience of off-campus study', PhD thesis, Geelong: Deakin

University. For a description of another approach to student organizations in distance education see, Williams, J and Williams, M (1987) 'A student-operated support network for distance learners', *International Council of Distance Education Bulletin* 13, 15–64.

5   This is not to accept her explanation as being the actual reason. It is also likely that problems to do with monitoring assessment and assessors (if latitude is extended to students to go beyond the set text and, therefore, the institution cannot control its educational technology as rigorously – see, for a broader analysis of such issues, Harris, D (1987) *Openness and Closure in Distance Education*, London: Falmer Press), the provision (or lack) of library facilities, and the concern to ensure a common foundation of understanding for subsequent courses, were also involved.

6   Ross Paul, who is President of Laurentian University in Canada – which is involved in open and distance education – has argued powerfully and eloquently that such organizations should be open in their management and organizational structures, strategies and principles and, consequently, throughout their everyday practices. See, Paul, R H (1990) *Open Learning and Open Management. Leadership and integrity in distance education*, London: Kogan Page – especially Chapter 6.

7   David Boud has made the point that, in effect, it should be interdependent learning which is the goal. For this and related matters see, Boud, D J (ed.) (1981), *Developing Student Autonomy in Learning*, London: Kogan Page. The references in notes 4 and 5 relate to this question. See also, Modra, H (1991) 'On the possibility of dialogue in distance education', in Evans, T D and King, B (eds) *Beyond the Text: Contemporary writing on distance education*, Geelong: Deakin University Press, pp 83–100.

Chapter 6

Work: the interplay between education, training and work

The personal, private and state investments in education are enormous in modern societies. Throughout this book there are examples of the cradle-to-the-grave nature of learning: lifelong learning. In various ways each chapter presents instances in the lives of people as they go about educating themselves. In this chapter the focus is on work and its relationship to education and training. Although important aspects of education cater for people's interests outside of work – Chapter 8 deals substantially with such interests for those who study later in life – it cannot be overlooked that a person's identity in society is usually closely interwoven with their paid work role in adulthood, and that education and training play crucial parts in developing people into their work roles. This is not to be confused with the narrow and instrumentalist education-for-work movement which has crept up alongside the economic rationalist cultures of many modern societies. The point is more that education provides people with a broad base of the knowledge, skills and values which are required for them to participate as citizens in societies where work is an almost inevitable feature of adult existence. It is impossible to imagine anyone living a life devoid of work, especially when one includes the unpaid labour which people contribute in and around the home, and the enormous amount of voluntary work performed in local, national and international communities. Both these forms of unpaid work are essential to keeping modern societies alive; however, in this chapter we shall be focusing on paid work.

The relationship between distance education and work is a long-established one.[1] Many people, especially teachers, have used forms of distance education to enhance their qualifications and develop their professional skills. Open education has come to the fore more recently as the basis for approaches to education and training in the workplace and for developing and providing courses which reflect industrial, professional or workplace needs and issues.[2] However, for the learners who wish to avail themselves of open and distance education to improve their work potential in some form, a concern remains about how to try and balance work and study (often with family responsibilities, too). This chapter explores these and related issues, using learners' stories.

Study for work

Many adults opt to study in order to enhance their work circumstances. This enhancement may be concerned with increasing employability, returning to work (which is especially the case for women, as is presented in Chapter 4), improving career and promotion opportunities, developing professional or occupational skills, changing jobs, etc. Essentially such students see courses as helping them either obtain a place (or 'better' place) in the paid workforce, or as improving their capacity to do their jobs. Sometimes employers specifically encourage people to enrol in courses, or they offer courses in their own education and training departments. Otherwise, the inducement to study for work is part of a broader social and political emphasis on such as being a desirable activity.

Rod, in his late 30s, 'retired' from teaching to develop and sell his skills in other parts of the labour market. He had engaged in a variety of courses in order to sustain and enhance his employability.

> I am constantly facing that problem of keeping up-to-date and in some ways keeping one step ahead of the job market. I go for interviews now and people are saying, 'What are you doing to keep up-to-date?'. If you can quote a relevant course it goes down extremely well.

> I didn't have a job to go to so, when I left teaching, I said I was retiring. But it is not so easy to retire from teaching. There are many advantages you give to and you get from teaching, and it is a career when all is said and done, rather than just a job.

> I tried anything and everything really. I went for a job with the probation service because I had worked there briefly in the past. I went for an

interview and they looked at my CV and said 'If you want some advice, train as a probation officer'. So I went to university full-time and trained as a social worker and probation officer. It took a year because I already had a relevant degree. So improving my qualifications through distance education from a certificate to a degree while I was teaching proved very useful. The entry qualification was a degree so, if I hadn't had that, I wouldn't have got over the first hurdle. I am sure my teaching career was particularly relevant.

After I qualified I would have liked to take up a position in the probation service, but there were no positions locally. I have returned to studying at a distance to complete my Honours, but it is going to be totally useless at the present time. I just hope that it will be useful when things pick up. At the moment I have several things on the go so I am well-employed now, but not anything to do with social work, more teaching really.

Rod's experience in the education and other labour markets had convinced him of the need to 'keep up-to-date' when he was in a job and of the need to keep 'one step ahead of the job market' when he was without a job. Another part of his story is covered in Chapter 2 (pages 31-2) and this illustrates that his 'retirement' from teaching was really more of a lifestyle and location change because he and his family decided they preferred to live in a remote area. This meant accepting a narrower and smaller job market and travelling substantial distances to obtain work.

Margaret was in her early 30s and had been studying for some years to obtain a degree. She had been outside the full-time workforce for several years, raising her children. She had worked in voluntary and paid part-time capacities while she was studying but, like Rod, she knew that to get a job she needed to be qualified. She was now considering completing another year of study to improve her chances of employment.

Honours should give me a few more options, but I am not quite sure.

Or I could do fourth year psychology and become listed as a psychologist. Perhaps I could do a Graduate Diploma qualification – in child development and psychology. I have talked to people within the college and they said that would be a reasonable qualification. It would give me the extra child development.

Margaret and Rod believed that education could make them more competitive in the labour market, but that qualifications alone would not actually create jobs for them. As Margaret was confronting her study options, there was a real sense of gamble and uncertainty. She was generally equally happy with the various educational options she could pursue – some of which would have been studied at a distance. She seemed equally happy with the sorts of job opportunities which may unfold. But the lack of a predictable correlation between any given qualification and a particular job created a real anxiety about what to choose for the best.

The choices for people already in work are much less likely to make them anxious. Although there is often not a predictable relationship between study and a better job, there is usually an increased chance – especially as the individual has some capacity to influence this relationship by applying for promotion, for example – and there is not the risk involved of not obtaining work because, of course, they are already employed.

People in work often choose to study, at least partly, to enhance the quality of the job they do and their career prospects. Such choices are not always made at the direct instigation of the employer. Paul worked for a customs and excise department and was enrolled in a distance education course.

> Computers interested me anyway; they did before work. So, I enrolled in the course partly out of interest but it is also very much work-orientated. I look after companies who are heavily into computers. It is a hell of a job, when talking to these guys if you can't talk their language. They fire things at me and I think 'Oh dear'! I have seen it happen, it is hopeless, it is chaos trying to do our job without some knowledge.

> I enjoy studying. I mean I wouldn't do it unless I enjoyed doing it, that is for sure and because it benefits work. Part of my job is talking to people. Job satisfaction makes a hell of a difference if you can talk to somebody in their language and they appreciate the answers you have been given. It makes life a lot more pleasant.

> I suspect I have been given jobs because I have got the expertise, there is no doubt about it. I have got a job now that I have been given because I have got this expertise.

Like many employers – partly, perhaps, because someone explicitly recognizes the benefits to the organization – Paul's department eventually provided valuable assistance.

> They wouldn't pay for the first year, I had to pay for that myself, to prove

I could do it. Once I did that they have paid towards my studies since. The Department are very good. They pay 80 per cent of my course fees, books, and give me several days special leave to study, attend exams, residential schools, etc.

They are selective now about which people and courses they will back. Years ago they paid for anyone to do anything, now they are getting more and more selective. I had no problems. Because it was computers, and maths and statistics and what have you, they said 'Yes please'! They are getting it cheap. Very cheap. I put the time in and they pay the fees.

There is a training and development section within the Department which monitors progress. I send them the results every year. They are very good as long as you are progressing; if you fail any – well, I am not sure what would happen. They may start questioning that.

Paul clearly sees a very important relationship between study and work. The relevance of his study to his work undoubtedly enhanced his job satisfaction. There was also a sense in which he enjoyed his course because it brought these other intrinsic benefits for him. However, he was less sure whether his studies would help him with promotion and career advancement.

I don't know. I suppose it must help in some ways because it proves I still have some drive left to do something like that. If I can keep studying for however many years it takes to get a degree I am going to prove I have still got some drive left. But there is nothing certain. If I get my degree at the end of the day they are not going to say 'Yes you can definitely have your promotion', not on that, because I know guys who have got degrees and got nowhere.

Paul's benefits from his studies are ones which are being accrued after several years in his career. In many respects, his studies are helping him position himself for the next phase in a career which is becoming increasingly involved with computer-related technologies. Marilyn provides a contrast. She is 19 years old and has commenced working as a trainee journalist on a country newspaper. She has been reporting on shows, court cases, notable weddings and deaths, etc. and sees for herself a future by moving into regional and national newspapers. In order to do so she enrolled in a journalism course which she could study at a distance.

Studying journalism is good. The practical side was especially good, because I don't get a lot of editorial guidance here. I appreciate some of the solid rules, the hard and fast rules which should apply. We studied ethics, the journalists' code of ethics, which was good for me to know. We have also compared media in different nations and although not as relevant to my present work, it was interesting and I guess it will help me make decisions for the future. The comparative course was mainly print media. There wasn't as much on television and radio, but as I am interested in travelling and the possibility of travelling in the job, or just travelling and trying to pick up a job overseas, it was interesting from that aspect.

Well [a senior person on a 'serious' national newspaper] has told me that if you have two journalists of equal writing skill and experience applying for a job, one has a degree and one hasn't, well the employer immediately goes for the one with the degree. Other people have told me 'Practical experience is just so important now, and there are radio and TV stations and papers just looking for a journalist with experience'. So, once again, I am leaving my options open by continuing with the degree and my job. I think that will all go well for me in the future. Just the fact that I have managed to study at a distance and made a start at it shows a bit of ambition and determination.

During next year I shall try to find another job on a regional daily or a suburban paper. I think I have learned as much as I will here, I have had almost two years. Probably by the time I get a job it could be two and a half or three years. I think that is enough. I am just getting a bit frustrated with management and lack of professionalism. There is no qualified journalist there sitting next to me who I can readily refer to, the sub-editor is just someone who walked into the job and the editor doesn't have a lot to do with the business. He doesn't offer much guidance. So for career reasons I just want to get somewhere that is organized and where I will be challenged a bit more and know that what I am doing is right.

Marilyn's increasing dissatisfaction with her job was substantially influenced by her course. As she learned more about journalism through her study, she was understanding more about how the experiences she was gaining at work were limited in both scope and quality. In this respect her studies were making her increasingly dissatisfied, whereas Paul was finding that his studies led to increasing job satisfaction within his customs work. Although Marilyn had some support from her employer, it was very limited in comparison with the assistance Paul received. This is probably symptomatic of the nature of the two organizations and their approaches to staff development and training.

As has been noted previously, one feature of contemporary societies is the increased demand for education and training on the part of employers. Degrees are now becoming – formally or informally – the basic entry qualification for many public and private sector organizations, and for those already within such organizations, a degree is often seen as a necessary – although not usually sufficient – qualification for promotion. The pressure is thus applied to employed people to enter into the 'qualifications chase' and what better way to do it than through open or distance education?! Anne, in her mid-40s, has taken this step in order to enhance her career prospects.

> Although these things go in troughs and peaks, companies and government departments have become more qualification-minded. Now in my particular field not many people have got degrees, but if you look at the advertisements for jobs, most of the jobs at my level and above require degrees of some kind. So it is not particularly important doing my course for my present job, but it is going to affect me moving to another position.

Craig is in his mid-20s and works in a government housing department in a provincial town. Like Anne, he is studying for a degree to enhance his future prospects.

> A degree just looks better for at least two or three career steps I want to take. It looks better for you to have a degree, plus there are more fields, professional fields, within housing administration which are becoming more welfare-orientated, so if you get a sociology or psychology background there will be more fields for me to go into.

> There are a lot of positions these days within housing administration where they say 'Degree desirable'. It means that if you haven't got one there is no way you are going to get the job.

Peter has found that now that he is in his mid-30s the working world around him is becoming increasingly graduate- or qualification-dominated.

> Within the next five years or so qualifications, especially degrees, are going to be more sought after both within government and private

enterprise. People who have human handling qualifications – not qualified psychologists, but those who have some understanding of it which enables them to be a better person manager – are going to be required. I have talked to other people and I have found that the police force now ask the applicants what studies they done. So that is one area where it is coming in. Over the last 18 months we have really started getting into a lot of psychological aspects of managing people, analysing people and dealing with everyday situations. So once that starts to become established, progression to requiring qualifications is just the next step.

Workers who contemplate becoming (part-time) learners in order to improve their career prospects and job satisfaction can see that they are also contributing to the gradual increase in the qualifications, knowledge and skills required for their jobs. The overall benefits to the workforce and employers may well be substantial; however, there remains the task of trying to fulfil the increased requirements.

Balancing work and study

Although work and study can be mutually beneficial, there are many tensions which most adult students have to resolve as they try to complete their studies and earn a living. Balancing work and study can be relatively easy if employers have policies for supporting study and put them into practice. However, for many students study is something which occurs outside of work as a private activity, and work has to be given its necessary priority. There are also the other balances between family and leisure activities – addressed especially within Chapters 4 and 7 – which need to be taken into account. Priorities are sometimes hard to balance, as Claire explains.

I was working full-time, so I thought a half credit course on brain biology and behaviour would be quite good. Also I thought I wouldn't find it too difficult because I am a sister in a theatre that does neurosurgery so, for the anatomy and physiology side of the brain, I had loads of surgeons at work to help me. Behaviour interests me anyway because I liked the bits of psychology I had done, so I didn't find that too hard. I was putting in about ten or eleven hours a week on my studies.

As I work shifts, I have no routine at all: my studying has to come last.

Husband, home, kids come first, job second and study last, unfortunately! But there is no way around it. The hardest thing I find is submitting assignments on time, which I never manage to do. I haven't got an assignment in on time yet.

Claire explained her difficulties with her husband's unwillingness to take his share of domestic and family responsibilities in Chapter 4 (pages 62–3). This means that her first priority was to fulfil her own and, in effect, most of her husband's responsibilities in this regard. Her second responsibility was to her work, and study, although it was partly related to her work, came third. Clearly, her late submission of assignments need be nothing more than a bureaucratic problem in the sense that assignment submission dates are generally set in the interests of the institution's schedule rather than the learners. Thus, if Claire's 'late' assignments were not late in terms of her own personal learning schedule, there would be no problem. Arguably, open education should be able to accommodate (or encourage) students working at their own pace. These paces will not be smooth and regular, but will accelerate and decelerate as work, family, illness and other factors come to bear.

The problem for students such as Claire who find that they are always falling behind the formal learning schedule applied by the institution, is that they develop a concept of themselves as learners which is at least partly negative. They can also fall out of synchronization with the institution's tutorial and other educational services, so they never obtain the full benefit from these. For example, broadcast or narrowcast radio and television programmes may have to be viewed before they are appropriate for some students' learning. Recording of programmes may help, but any interactive elements to these programmes will be lost and, of course, the pacing aspect, while positive for those students who are able to keep on (the institution's) schedule, is a further reminder of their problems for those who cannot. Perhaps students should endeavour to make these problems their teacher or trainer's concerns; however, as was shown in Chapter 5, this is rarely easy.

Michael didn't have to worry about support from his employer to complete his studies: he was his employer. Michael ran his own Karate school (dojo) and could make his own decisions about when he worked and studied. However, maintaining the balance was not easy and sometimes proved to be so difficult that he felt guilty about obligations he was unable to fulfil.

When I was out for the study school it was at the same time as opening

> my dojo. I had an important overseas visitor – a very high karate instructor – to participate in the opening. It was just too much. Over three weeks I had to complete my activities at the study school and then at night time study and prepare for the next day. Alongside this was the opening of my dojo here. This visitor was across for that week and I had to spend time with him. So we had one day and night out together. I felt very much ill at ease because I should have spent more time with him. I explained to him that I just couldn't: I had to do these studies. I didn't realize that the study school was so compact and so comprehensive.

Michael's problem was one which occurred partly because he didn't understand the requirements of the study school. It was a compulsory part of his psychology course so he was unable to complete the course without it. The opening of his new dojo was an important step for his livelihood and it was something which he had planned for well in advance, but he couldn't avoid the clash between study and work. In contrast, Peter's problems were brought about by a natural disaster: a massive bushfire which killed and injured people in his area and destroyed many homes and other properties. As a member of a government housing department, he was working to counsel, accommodate and rehouse people rendered homeless by the fires. Suddenly, his work became a serious and all-consuming priority.

> I have had to defer a couple of units because of work pressures. The first time was during the bushfires. I was working all hours setting up caravans down there, making sure people had money to buy the necessities, apart from what they were being given by the Red Cross and other welfare organizations. It was personally and physically very demanding and my studies were completely out of my mind. I deferred again last semester because it was just getting too hectic at work. I would come home too drained to be able to concentrate on my studies.

Michael's studies were connected to his Karate business development, but this does not mean that the pace of his learning could be changed to suit changes in workload at work or, especially, crises. The onward march of the term and semester is relentless in most educational institutions. Possibilities for extensions to assignments and deferments of studies are really only minor adaptations which are made to students' needs. Several open learning courses, often offered outside of 'traditional' educational institutions, provide for students to enrol and complete their studies on a rolling basis throughout the year.[3] This has considerable advantages for independent learning, but has severe drawbacks for approaches to teaching and learning which rely upon or enable group learning in some form.

Group learning commitments, such as tutorials and study schools, provide a constant source of difficulties for students who have to balance work and learning. Anne often missed tutorials because her job took her away from home.

> I go to various cities and towns for my work. Not so much now, but I had to travel a fair bit then for things like meetings, particularly, meetings and courses. This meant I couldn't always attend the study groups and tutorials.

> This year because I would have one unit left over, I decided I didn't want it to drag on, so I have taken three units this semester, which has nearly killed me. I found that very difficult. But I did get some time off work – study leave – because one of the units was not available through distance education, so I had to attend lectures and tutorials during the day. I managed to get some study leave, which I haven't had before because, if your course is available outside the normal hours, you can't get study leave. So if you study through distance education, as I have, you miss out.

Anne's work commitments really only had a minor effect on her studies, because the study groups and tutorials were optional activities for students studying at a distance. She generally managed to balance study and work, even to the extent of completing in her final semester what is equivalent to three-quarters of a full-time study load, although with the assistance of some study leave. Craig found that he could adjust his work slightly in order to be able to get to tutorials at the end of the day and he could rely on his mother to help out too!

> It wasn't a hassle to get to the evening classes. I just worked through my lunch and then I could leave work at 4.20 pm, go to a class and then come home for dinner. I study in the evenings and weekends sometimes. When I have an assignment to hand in, I don't post it. My mother usually hands them in for me on the morning they're due. I have got to get to work, so she goes down there and hands them in.

Paul found that he could balance study and work readily.

> It isn't too bad, I used to get into the office at 9 so the morning was a nice time to study. We were fairly used to getting up early – 5.30 or 6.00. It

wasn't that much of a strain studying at that time before going to work. It was all right. Work went in around it, it was no problem.

Paul's case represents one of the better circumstances for the working student. As we have seen, balancing work and study – often alongside other responsibilities such as those connected with the family – is often problematic for students. At particular times, it is not unusual to find that the difficulties of maintaining a balance are such that studies have to be jettisoned temporarily or other responsibilities compromised. It is difficult to assess exactly the consequences of this virtually continuous balancing process on learners and their learning. Certainly, there is evidence that they are occasionally (or more frequently) finding it impossible to spend the time on their studies which they feel they really need, and this leads to assignments being submitted late, etc. Studies of students who withdraw from their courses also show that work-related pressures are a common reason for such withdrawals.[4] The problems learners face in balancing work and study are important ones to be recognized, understood and addressed by open and distance educators.

Education at work

One context in which one might expect that balancing work and study would be less of a problem is where the education takes place in the workplace. However, while this is generally the case, as usual with any human endeavour, matters are rarely as simple as they seem at first sight.

Increasingly, in industrialized nations, companies are seeking to enhance their efficiency, productivity, competitiveness and quality through, in part, improvements to the knowledge, skills and values of employees. Open and distance education principles, practices and institutions have become part of this process as companies appreciate that a mix of work-based education and independent learning using course materials affords a good balance between employee and employer investment in education and training. Rather than the employer being virtually the total investor in education and training through the provision of courses on-site and during work-time, and rather than the employees assuming the total investment, as has been the case with most of the students' stories we have seen previously in this chapter, there is a realization that a blend of workplace and open or distance education can bring together a more equal investment. A more equal investment, in terms of time and money, also means that the learners have fewer problems balancing study and work because, to a large degree, the balance has been struck. George is a regional training manager for a large multinational manufacturing company.

> We became involved in developing a course specifically designed for our production operators. We negotiated with the College to develop a course which would get credit towards a certificate which they validated but which was specifically designed for our industry – this company in particular. This was part of an overall strategy to ensure that our plants are world-competitive. We are developing several courses in this way and other companies are beginning to take notice.
>
> On the day we launched the course the Managing Director addressed the production workers – the production line was stopped which, in this company, means it is serious. We gave each worker a brochure and an audiocassette explaining the new course. The idea was that they could play the tape in the car. It was then up to them to volunteer. The message was clear. If they wanted to get on in the Company, they needed to improve their knowledge and skills. The certificate would make it legitimate and, although we didn't actually make anything of this, it gives them a piece of paper which they can use for other jobs in the industry outside the Company.
>
> The idea was that there would be a designed course and course materials which we worked-up with the College. So it was very much a course designed for this Company, with actual company examples, etc., but which fitted with the academic requirements of the College and had the sort of material they required, too. The Company picks up the costs of course development, books, tutoring, etc. and provides some work time for study (usually at the beginning or end of a shift). The employee has to attend some sessions in their own time and also has to study at home with the course materials.

Open and distance educators and their institutions have a lot to contribute in these sorts of circumstances. There is a powerful capacity to blend their approaches with the education and training needs of companies and organizations. For the learners, there is the benefit of having the educational quality which an open or distance education institution can provide, matched with the curriculum which will specifically benefit them in their employment careers. Matthew is a student on a course such as the one George described above.

I was attracted to the course to upgrade my qualifications. It does mean that I get a certificate eventually. In this day and age, who knows what is going to happen with jobs? So I reckon I shall be better off with a qualification.

Susan had a similar view.

It's good to have a qualification, but I'm also interested in learning more about the technical side behind our work. There are certainly increasing demands from the Company to do courses.

Mario saw this in more global terms.

The way the world is going with all this new technology, everyone is having to change and adapt. Well, if you don't keep up you're in trouble. The pace of the job is changing, too. I need this course to help me keep up.

There is not room here to do more than note the emergence of these sorts of changes to the ways open and distance education are being used in the workplace. They provide a glimpse of an emerging sector of the student community which needs to be studied further to understand the teaching and learning implications. Some of the difficulties of the relationships between study and work which the previous students outlined in this chapter are less likely to occur with courses which are jointly developed between industries and open or distance education organizations. For example, there are likely to be clearer relationships between studying and career paths, less clashes between work and study schedules and commitments, and better support for learning – both in the form of workplace tuition or mentoring, and in the form of financial provision towards course costs.

However, other tensions also come to bear when another significant factor, in this case an industry, is added to the educational 'equation'. Certain degrees of curriculum and pedagogical freedom are relinquished by the educational institution in order to allow the industry to say what is to be learned and how. Therefore, students' freedom to choose their courses is also likely to be reduced and learning 'for its own sake' is still likely to remain something which occurs outside of open or distance education in the workplace. There are other constraints, too. The selection and sponsoring of students is something which the industry is likely to control or influence significantly. Some employees may be dragooned into courses, others may volunteer. Some employees may regret they were not chosen, others may regret that they were. There are several other issues which exist, however, in this important area of development which have concerned open and distance educators. These require further exploration and critical analysis in terms of both learners' and employers' needs and contexts.

In a sense the relationship between education and work is being reversed. In the industrialized world, education, especially schooling, has been an important precursor to work. Education and work have long been involved together in the 'sandwich'-course sense of people sequentially being in work and attending educational institutions (apprenticeships are a good example). Now we are seeing work becoming increasingly a place for education. Not necessarily in the sense that all the education physically takes place at the worksite, but rather, as has been shown briefly here, education taking place in the context of work for the learner/employee. The open and distance educator or trainer who becomes engaged in this emerging area of activity is likely to experience interesting times. On the basis of the students' stories that are told in this book, it will be very important to come to understand the learners in those contexts, not just as employees, but as people with family, social, educational and other concerns.

Notes

1　Geoffrey Bolton's article 'The opportunity of distance' (1986) *Distance Education*, 7, 1, 5–22) is a good starting point for understanding the long relationship between distance education and the development of economic and employment opportunities in emerging societies. It can also be argued that, historically, the development of distance education is entwined with the provision of teacher education for teachers who were posted to developing rural and remote areas; see, for example, Evans, T D and Nation, D E (1993) 'Educating teachers at a distance in Australia: some history, research results and recent trends', in Perraton, H (ed.) *Distance Education for Teacher Training*, London: Routledge, pp. 261–86. Hilary Perraton's opening chapter, 'The context' (pp. 1–17) in this book, also provides some important detail on this matter. Of course, such teachers were placed in remote and rural areas to contribute to the rising generation's potential for developing the social, economic and cultural fabric of the societies. Much the same pattern between distance education, teacher education and development can be seen in contemporary developing nations. See, for example, the chapters by Kwasi Ansu-Kyeremeh – 'Distance education in a developing context: Ghana', and Richard Guy – 'Distance education and the developing world' in Evans, T D and King, B (eds) (1991) *Beyond the Text: Contemporary writing on distance education*, Geelong: Deakin University Press.

2   See, for examples, Peter Bowen's chapter, 'Open learning formats in high performance training' and Tom Foggo's chapter, 'The introduction of open learning as a change process', in Tait, A (ed.) (1993) *Key Issues in Open Learning*, Harlow: Longman. Also, for other writing in the field, see Paine, N (ed.) *Open Learning in Transition*, Cambridge: National Extension College, and Temple, H (1991) *Open Learning in Industry*, Harlow: Longman.

3   Empire State College in New York State is one of the best known examples of a 'traditional' educational institution which endeavours to provide this sort of flexibilty. It also has other 'open' education features to its operations which set it apart from its counterpart institutions. Dan Granger's chapter, 'Reflections on curriculum as process' in Evans, T D and Nation, D E (eds) (1993) *Reforming Open and Distance Education*, London: Kogan Page, discusses the work on the Empire State College in relation to the Open University in this regard. James Hall, the President of Empire State College has also written extensively about the College and the issues behind its work in his book published in 1991, *Access through Innovation*, New York: American Council on Education & Macmillan.

4   I have uncovered this finding myself in evaluations and also in communicating with students who have, or are about to, withdraw. I have published the findings of one such study of people who withdrew from a distance education course; see Evans, T D (1991) 'An evaluation of classroom processes', in, Altrichter, H, Evans, T D and Morgan, A R, *Windows: Research and evaluation on a distance education course*, Geelong: Deakin University Press, pp. 139–73.

Chapter 7

Play/time: study as leisure or the loss of leisure?

People segment their daily lives into work, family and domestic life, and leisure. In previous chapters, aspects of family (parenting) and working lives have been considered in relation to several students' stories of their experiences and views. In this chapter the place that students' learning takes in their leisure time is the focus.

For most adults, their waking hours during the week are largely given to paid work, domestic work and parenting. What little time is left may be used for leisure activities, such as reading newspapers and magazines, listening to music or watching television. Weekends afford more time for most adults when other leisure activities typically come to the fore, for example, sports, gardening or visiting relatives or friends. The task of managing daily life is not easy. Juggling time between one's various commitments, responsibilities and interests often requires the skill of an acrobat! Perhaps it is astounding that so many adults elect to dedicate some of their leisure time to studying, especially by open or distance education where immense self-discipline is required and so little student peer-group pressure or support applies. Yet it is very clear that, around the world, millions of adults do commit their leisure time to learning, and an increasing proportion of these adults, especially women, complete most of their studies in their private worlds of home.[1]

Leisure is about recreation, that is the re-*creation* of one's physical, psychological, intellectual (some would add spiritual) selves. Some of this is playful. People play games and sports to give their minds and bodies the chance to gambol and cavort in ways in which the constraints of everyday life do not allow. They use dance and drama to project themselves into roles and experiences which allow fantasy, performance and discipline to be explored. They collect the collectables and, in so doing, study and calculate their essence and worth. In most, if not all leisure activities, there emerges a level of personal engagement and understanding which is akin to that which is used in formal education. Indeed, many leisure activities, quite apart from their other pleasurable qualities, can be seen as a form of self-education or independent learning.

Educators and trainers could benefit from dwelling on the learning which people ordinarily pursue in their lives as part of their leisure. People who are avid followers of football teams, for example, can often recount facts and figures from their teams' histories with surprising accuracy and can comment on the strategies and performances of recent games with analytical skill. The demonstrations of horticultural knowledge, skill and artistry by home gardeners can be astounding, as can the relevant skills of those who weave, embroider, woodwork, photograph and so forth. Most people have considerable capacities for self-education and independent learning which are largely unrecognized by themselves, let alone educators and trainers.

Self-education or independent learning in this sense – if not all senses – is not really independent in the solitary sense. All knowledge can be seen as social in the sense that it is created and stored (partly) by and in people. Therefore, learning is something which needs to tap into this social resource in some way. Even the forms of leisure-based learning which have been mentioned here are mediated in much the same sorts of ways in which open and distance education are mediated. The media used include print (such as in gardening or photography magazines, or in embroidery patterns, sports books, etc.), radio, television, computer and audiocassette. There seems to be much to be learned by open and distance educators and trainers from understanding these 'learners'. It appears that, in practice, there may not be a great deal of difference between learning informally and learning formally for leisure. However, symbolically and institutionally there are probably very significant differences which keep these two types of learning separate in the minds of most people. As has been evident throughout this book, the students' stories come from people who are studying formally through structured education or training, rather than through informal self-education. This chapter is no exception.

The relationship between education and recreation is not often explored, unlike the relationship between education and work, and yet in open and distance education most learners are contributing a significant proportion of their leisure time to their studies. Previously it has been noted that people in general commit a proportion of their leisure time to learning knowledge and skills which contribute to their recreation. Taking open and distance students, why do they choose to spend their leisure time (or, at least a proportion of it) on formal study? Do they see education as a leisure activity: a form of *re-creation*? Or is education seen as an intrusion into leisure time: another chore or form of work?

Playtime: education as leisure

The answers to the above questions are not unequivocal. For some people the pursuit of educational activities is a pleasure, is playful and is recreational. For others it is worthwhile work to be performed during time they would normally have allocated to leisure. For still others it is more of a necessary chore which needs to be completed in order to obtain a qualification or access to other things they perceive as worthwhile. In this section we shall consider those who fall into the first of these general areas.

June's studies in the area of art were congruent with an important part of her recreational interests. She embraced her courses and made them part of her family's leisure activities.

> I studied the Renaissance and Reformation periods and then I followed-up with a course on art history. I really enjoyed it. During those years I took the family to Italy for holidays. We used to go for a month, so we went all around Venice and Florence. All around various other places and I would take my books and course materials to look up things I needed. I think we all benefited because I talked about things with the children and showed them things. They were becoming as interested as me. I think art is quite a family thing really, you tend to look at sculpture and paintings and things, and discuss them together. I also had pictures around the walls at home from my course.

June's artworks from her course displayed on her walls symbolized the belonging that her study activities had in the home. This is reminiscent of the ways young children's drawings at kindergarten and primary school are displayed on their parents' and grandparents' refrigerator doors and the like. David's views on study as recreation also provide a lens through which we can view the meaning of June's pictures and her family's holidays.

Study has broadened my intellect. Whereas I would sum up the situation very quickly, right or wrong, I don't do that any longer. I will sit back and think a bit, look at it from all sides. I have always had an interest in art, but I can now look *into* not *onto* a painting or piece of sculpture or whatever it might be and appreciate it more. I have given up a lot to do it, and the return has been worth it.

When we look *into* June's comment we can see that it was not just a case of the family legitimating her study as a worthwhile activity for her to pursue, rather as children's early drawings are displayed as a legitimation of their learning to draw and express themselves visually. June's study had become more than this: it was now a family pleasure and recreation. Her study had even become family education, too. In such settings, and for such people, education does not just occur, especially in its leisure forms, as something which emanates from educational organizations. For these people, other aspects of their lives are educative and they practise self-education in the more literal sense of the term discussed previously, rather than as it is used in educational circles. Of course, formal education may provide an impetus or framework with which they continue their self-education, whether in the art galleries, national parks, libraries or any one of the other cultural resources of our time.

David's view was that he had given up a lot to look *into* works of art. He had chosen to sacrifice some things he had enjoyed in order become equipped to understand things differently.

I gave up league snooker, which I enjoyed thoroughly. I sang at the cathedral and they are very high-powered in the choir. I sang there for 18 years. I gave that up. I was on the church council and one or two other committees and that sort of thing and I have given those up. In fact, I have given up everything, but what I have obtained from my courses has been worth it.

It is tempting to think of people who study for pleasure as being in some ways less serious about their study. But this seems to be missing the point. If they were studying for work – perhaps on some training programme to enhance their skills – they would take it seriously as work. When people study for leisure it seems they are often looking for something even deeper. They want something to change the ways they see the world, think about the world, talk about the world and write about the world. For David to jettison 18 years of serious choral music for a course, he had to be creating for himself something even more important and personally significant.[2]

Nick showed a similar commitment to education as a worthwhile activity. He seemed to be looking for something better to do with *his* time.

> My studies don't affect my leisure activities a great deal. The first year I studied I used to play the guitar. But when I got into the course I put the guitar into the loft and didn't touch that for six months. I avoid watching television. I used to go for a drink and do lots of weight training. I had lots of hobbies. I am not one for sitting around doing nothing or watching television. There are better things to do than that. I found that is largely the extent of the sacrifice I make for studying. Very often I am sitting studying and I think, 'Will I watch telly? Better not – got to get it done'.

Nick seemed to find the lure of television quite seductive, but his studies were something he wanted for himself so much that he resisted the temptation. This is a common theme with certain students – not just the lure of television, but also of other activities which they found less worthwhile. Amy, as a retired person, had more leisure time than she had when she was working. Study was something she chose to do to make good use of her new-found recreational time.

> Studying has actually got in the way of some of the things I wanted to do. Only recreational things, like concerts, plays, taking part in things and taking my grandchildren out. Also, going away sometimes, going to stay with friends and so on. I feel as if I am stuck here because there is a tutorial coming or an essay due in or whatever.

> Study keeps me out of mischief. There has been a great big campaign going on here to try and keep the school open. I could have got involved with that – carrying banners and making speeches and all that. By studying I did something quietly at home. I thought that would be the sensible thing to do. I could have gone on having a rip-roaring time in Spain, couldn't I? Or something silly like that? But there is no point in that. There are all sorts of silly things you can do. You can get involved – and I certainly wouldn't want to – with the Darby and Joan Club here!

Amy saw education as something which was a worthwhile recreational pursuit for her: it was not 'silly'. However, we can see that trying to keep all her various leisure interests in balance was not easy, but her commitment to her study was very high. It was as if her study had become a core of her life which provided some external connection and legitimation. It was a bit like work in these respects, although without some of its more arduous and repetitive daily demands.

Once embarked on an open or distance education course for recreational purposes, there are occasions when the prescribed activities spill over into other regions of students' lives. The demands which educational institutions impose upon the lives of the students can occur in ways and to degrees which mean they can no longer use their normal recreational times at evenings and weekends to fulfil their study obligations. Examinations and residential schools are the most common examples. In these instances, some students choose to take their annual holidays (that is, another form of leisure time) to attend residential schools. William found this to be quite appropriate for him.

> Residential schools were not a problem for me, apart from it taking up a week of my annual leave, but that is one of those things. I put my name down at work in good time so they are quite happy about it, they don't seem to mind. If there is an exam I usually arrange for some holidays at that time as well, either a couple of days or I will take a week at the end of October when I have got an exam. I will take a week off prior to the exam and the actual day of the exam. I get five weeks holidays and I spend up two of those weeks on my studies.

With both Amy and William there is a positive view about the use of their leisure time for their study. There is the message with both that sometimes there are competing things they would like to do with their time, but they choose to let their study take precedence. As is shown in the next section, for some students study is not so much leisure – a chosen form of recreation – but a loss of their leisure for something which they need or want to do, but do not see as leisure or recreation in itself.

No time to play: education as the loss of leisure

Students who find that study is something which intervenes in their leisure lives in ways which they find difficult, are often studying for career-related reasons. They have usually chosen to study for themselves, perhaps with encouragement to do so by others. However, their decision is not as something for their own pleasure, but for career enhancement in some respect. Marilyn is a cadet journalist and is studying a journalism course in her spare time. She finds that both her job and her study are mixed up with her leisure.

My employer has encouraged me to get involved in the community, and I think that is only right, too. That is the way you find out as a journalist about how the place ticks and, of course, you meet people and make friends. I joined the Young Farmers Club when I first came, just to meet people. It is a struggling club, we haven't got many members and this year there was nobody else to take on the job of president so I was it. I am also the public relations officer for the district council. It is my own choice to get involved in community life because I enjoy it and my employers encouraged me to do so as well.

It has been difficult, to fit my studies in. I am not sure if it's my age, that makes it that way. I suppose what you need is the determination to do the work, but the fact that I am the president of the Young Farmers Club here, and I have church choir practice and I play basketball and I am involved with the church youth group and a committee there, makes it more difficult. It is bad enough when you come home from work and you have got to sit down and study, but when you have perhaps two or three nights out a week, doing these various things, it makes it even more difficult and, especially, when you want to have a bit of a social life with friends. You are often torn between study and doing something with them.

Time is what it's about. The night before my last two essays were due in I spent half the night sleeping and half working in two hour blocks just to get it done. I think my problem is leaving things to the last minute, which I never did at school. It just seems to have been something that has happened this year. I have a chapter of work to do each week, well, I might get behind a couple of times with that and think I will catch it up next week, but I don't and so I am left with a bit of a backlog in the last couple of weeks. It's all stops out then to get everything finished, but one weekend, 2 o'clock on both Saturday and Sunday afternoons, I sat down to study and had visitors both times. One was a friend who just needed to talk about something, and you can't say 'This is my study time, go away' when they need to talk. I put friendships and being able to help people ahead of academic achievements at the moment. I think that is right. So it is mainly the time factor, and I have just resigned myself to the fact that I will probably only get credits. It will be my own fault.

Marilyn is clearly not driven to study because she finds it one of the things she would most like to do with her time. Her motivation stems from her work and, therefore, she seems to see study as a necessary responsibility connected with her work. She blames herself for not organizing her time better, but really she does not want to do any differently with her time: she would just rather that she somehow managed to complete her studies more readily and more successfully. We can contrast her with the students in the previous section in that Marilyn conveys the feeling that she sees her study as an extension of her work into her leisure time. She calls aspects of the study requirements 'work' – as in, 'I have a chapter of work to do each week'. It seems quite appropriate that she does so in that this is a course directly geared to her chosen career.

Craig, likewise, was a young person at the beginning of his career who was studying because he felt he ought to do so. He also felt guilty about the way he had approached his studies.

> I haven't really put in the work this year, so if I do fail this year it will be my own fault. It'll be because I had two or three things going at once, and it is also fairly hard working and studying. I have just started martial arts, amateur radio and I am helping with a band, so my weekends are gone. Because of this I was unprepared for the exam and that is why I am really worried about it. I know that next time I might have to repeat it, and I shall have to do more work.

As can be seen, Craig had taken on several leisure activities while he was studying. The considerable lure of leisure activities, especially for single people like Marilyn and Craig, seems evident. This lure seems particularly powerful when the activities are ones which are conducted with friends and peers. Craig's story suggests that he saw studying as something different from, or perhaps between, both his work and leisure. As a consequence, he had not found the time to study his course sufficiently or to revise properly for his exams. He was interviewed the evening after he had sat the examination and he was convinced he was going to fail. He was unsure whether he would be able to just resit the examination, or have to repeat the whole course the next year. He was preparing himself to readjust his leisure commitments so that he could study more conscientiously during the next year.

Steve was in a similar position to Craig with regard to the way he viewed his studies, but rather than take on new activities, he dropped some.

> Sometimes I can't do as much sport as I would like to do. I suppose study affects my social life a bit. I obviously have to think more about whether I have got study to do and if it has to be done and can't be put off. Study does affect my social life.

Steve is resigned to the view that his studies require sufficient priority for success. His social life could suffer if necessary, perhaps because he thought he would be able to resurrect it later during the holidays or after he had completed his course. Steve is a few years older than Craig and Marilyn, and he has a partner. He is a pharmacist and is studying his course for his own personal interest. So, in a sense, his study is his leisure and he is merely adjusting his priorities within this aspect of his life in order to complete it.

Paul was less involved in leisure pursuits before he commenced studying and so the sacrifice was relatively minor for him. He is able to allocate time to his study because he believes he is not someone who has to lose many leisure pursuits.

> I still manage the odd game of cricket, playing once a week during the summer. I still manage that. I can't think of anything I actually had to give up. I have never gone down the pub as a rule. The evenings were either out in the garden or sat in front of the television, so I wasn't giving up a hell of a lot.

For Paul, it is merely some readjustment to his gardening and television watching – neither of which he seemed to cherish anyway – which gave him the time for study. For some students their commitments to their leisure activities are such that they make firm decisions in their lives to either keep their study limited or to curtail other activities. Gwynneth took the former approach.

> I restrict my studies to one course at a time. I think I can only manage one course and live as well. I don't want to lose friends and family contacts; they are all very important. To push them all to one side to study is foolish. If you need to do it for some specific important purpose maybe that is different, but my particular reason for studying is almost entirely for self-gratification.

Gwynneth's approach is another form of balancing the leisure time (and other forms of time) in her life. She controls the pace of her study to suit her interests. Educational administrators and government bureaucrats often dislike the length of time it takes for some part-time students to complete their courses. However, for those with a commitment to open education or to students having control over their own learning, it is difficult to reject Gwynneth's approach as unacceptable. Indeed, some may even commend it as being a measured and balanced approach to studying. Bureaucrats tend not to like the slow completion rates which this entails, but for the learners it is good that they make their choices carefully and strike their own balances.

Lyn took the position that she would forgo work for a year in order to maintain her other leisure activities alongside her studies.

> I was just generally busy last semester and I was a bit frazzled. I decided I would have this year off work. I thought that I would indulge myself and do things that I hadn't had time to do before when I was trying to work and study. I wanted to visit a few friends or have lunch out occasionally or go and see a couple of films, or do more gardening. In fact I didn't do any of those things. Housework and other things absorbed the extra time so I felt it was a bit of a waste of the year; it was just as well I was studying and had that to show for it.

It appears that Lyn also sees study as something between work and leisure. She also shows the problem which so many students face of finding that their plans went astray. Students should be realistic about their plans and regularly review their 'balance' between study and other aspects of their lives.

Telling time: a final comment

People who choose to engage in open and distance education do so for a variety of reasons and in so doing they necessarily make adjustments to the time they allocate to other activities in order to accommodate study. Depending on the length and duration of the course they have undertaken, the consequences of this re-balancing of their time might be minor or major. For many it is an undertaking which goes well beyond a single year, which they understand at the outset. However, understanding the broad nature of the commitment is one thing, and sustaining it each day for such a long period is another.

Students' stories of their studies often exhibit the view that events did not unfold in the ways they had anticipated. Invariably, this has meant that they find that allocating sufficient time to study, or balancing it appropriately with other aspects of their lives, leads to stresses and strains. It is not simply a matter of understanding the workload and commitments to examinations, tutorials, etc., although this is important. Rather, it is a matter of telling time as a dynamic entity, in the sense that the various requirements of a course have different implications for individual students, depending upon the ways they come to study and upon the interactive effects of their other time commitments. In this way, it is not possible to predict with any certainty the time it will take for any given student to complete a course of study. It is possible to make assessments of reading times, typical amounts of time on activities, or listening to tapes, etc. But the total impact of these items, which are exacerbated by the chaotic nature of individuals' lives, means that time predictions are risky ventures.

Notes

1 Margaret Grace and I have written about the 'privatization' of learning through distance education as something which is gendered, in the sense that women are particularly disposed to using distance education in their private worlds at home. This is not just about time, but also place: the home being the private world of women into which distance education is projected. See Evans, T D and Grace, M (1994) 'Distance education and the gendered privatisation of learning', *Journal of Curriculum Studies* (in press).

2 This point is borne out, although sometimes indirectly, in research into why people choose to study. Such research deals with students' orientations to study which draw the distinction between those who have rather extrinsic motives (seeking a grade, qualification, promotion or pay rise, for example) and those who have intrinsic motives (seeking understanding, personal competence, etc.). Alistair Morgan discusses this work in his book in this series, Morgan, A R (1993) *Improving Your Students' Learning*, London: Kogan Page. Research on school teachers studying professional qualifications at a distance, whom one might have felt were most imbued with the intrinsic values of education, shows that many are prone to using all their educators' skills to 'beat the system' and complete their course with a minimum of effort. See, Evans, T D and Nation, D E (1991) 'Distance education and teachers' professional development', in Hughes, P (ed.) *Teachers' Professional Development*, Melbourne: Australian Council for Educational Research, pp. 114–28. David Harris gives a wonderful example of a teacher he interviewed as part of his research on the UK Open University, who used a variety of tactics to minimize his efforts; he even pointed to unopened envelopes containing sections of course materials for a course he had already passed! See, Harris, D (1987) *Openness and Closure in Distance Education*, London: Falmer Press, pp. 112–13.

Chapter 8

Age: learning in retirement

The changing nature of work in recent years has contributed not only to changes in the work which is performed and its organization at the workplace, at national and global levels, but it has also contributed to the nature and organization of those who are outside paid work. For the young, this has typically meant an increase in school and post-school full-time education, and a reduction in apprenticeships and jobs. For those who have been in work for three decades or so, there has been an increase in redundancy (both compulsory and voluntary) and, depending on their age, increased opportunities for early retirement. Some occupations, such as the police and military, have 'early' retirements as a normal feature of their work and staff organization. For most workers, however, retirement has usually been something which was only available at a prescribed age in their later life (and often with a difference between men and women – ironically those with the greater life expectancy, women, having the lower retirement ages).

Nowadays, in the developed world, it is not uncommon to hear of people in their 50s retiring from occupations which they would previously have stayed in until between age 60 and 65. Statistically, such people have another third of their lives left to live and this has contributed to 'lifelong education' becoming a substantial feature of the educational landscape. Open and distance education have emerged as important ways in which people can sustain their education as *lifelong*. People of the 'traditional' retirement ages enrol in distance education courses to study things that they have not had the time or opportunity to do during their working and parenting lives. Now, with people retiring earlier and with the expansion in open education opportunities, we can see people taking courses not only to fulfil long-held educational desires and ambitions, but also to obtain skills and knowledge which enable them to work – paid or voluntary – in occupations or activities which sustain their lifestyles and livings.

In this chapter stories from learners who have undertaken courses after retirement are presented which reveal some of the key issues which confront them as learners. These stories are ones which may help those in a similar position to create their own lifelong learning and also provide educators with insights for their consideration.

Retiring for a future

Work is usually seen as the activity performed to provide people's livelihoods. It is often portrayed as something which is a necessary evil which must be endured during the week for the weekends, during the year for the holidays and during a lifetime for retirement. Fortunately, some people derive enjoyment and pleasure from their work as well as from the income they earn. Work, however, is also an important anchor in human life to the extent that, in industrialized nations in particular, human identity is inextricably connected to occupation. It is this factor which often works against women, as we saw in Chapter 4, some of whom find that being outside the workforce and 'just a housewife' is not sufficient to be 'fulfilled'.

Retirement is usually viewed in positive terms by older people. They see this as an opportunity to spend time on some of the things that they have been unable to do during their previous years due to their work and family commitments. There is also the uncertainty about what retirement will really be like and there seems to be a strong desire for people to plan activities for their retirement so that they know they will be gainfully occupied. Education is often one such consideration and the advantages of open and distance education appeal to many retirees.

One of the emerging opportunities in what can be see as a form of open education is the University of the Third Age – usually abbreviated to U3A. This is a non-profit volunteer organization which offers courses using principally retirees as voluntary tutors based on the needs of the learners (again, principally retirees) and the skills and capacities of the tutors. The cost to the learners is minimal in the form of a membership fee and a subscription for each course to cover expenses. Madge explained that she started with U3A because of a friend.

John was tutoring a U3A class in philosophy – he's very interested in philosophy, he used to be a school teacher, English, I think. Anyway, he suggested I consider a class. I think I had said I wanted to learn more about computers because my grandchildren were always playing on theirs and they'd say 'C'mon Nan, have a go' but I cannot even work out what I'm supposed to do. They explain it in a whizz, too fast for me to understand. Anyway, John said, 'Oh we have courses on computers at U3A why don't you come along?' Well, I decided to have a go at something, but not computers. I did a local history course. Do you know, it was fascinating. We even went on field trips, just walking mostly, looking at buildings and things. But it was really good. I have enrolled to do an introductory computer course next. It's in the evenings so we can use the local school's computers. I prefer things in the daytime, but we can't do it because the children are using the computers at school. That's fair enough.

For people such as Madge, open education courses which are not part of any formal award are often just what they require. They learn for their own sake and get the opportunity for social contacts that they lose from not being at work. Although these sorts of classes from organizations and local authorities cover a wide range of interests — from car maintenance and cooking, to politics and psychology — there is often a view from the participants that they are deliberately avoiding certain sorts of activities which are often planned for the elderly. Stan makes such a point.

There's a bit of a view that activities for the elderly are bingo, carpet bowls and a Christmas do. We want to show that we can think and that we need intellectual stimulation, not just being left to vegetate in some old folks' club.

Some retirees exercise even more demanding educational choices. They undertake courses to complete the Year 12 or Sixth Form education they missed decades before. Others choose to study various forms of tertiary education courses through to higher degrees. In these cases they are immersed in a student population which spans one or two generations and they enter courses which were not specifically designed with older students' learning skills and life experiences in mind.

David is a retired bank manager who had sustained an interest in psychology for some years. On his retirement he enrolled in an Arts degree and chose as his first course one which covered philosophy, literature and psychology. He was in his element.

After years of banking it was as if I had been unleashed. I was very nervous about my first assignment, I guess I was dreading failing, I don't know how I would have handled that. However, it didn't come to pass – sorry! – I got a Distinction. This was for an essay on Existentialism. I just loved it. We had to read Sartre and Camus, you know, *The Plague*. I thought it was fascinating. I studied the course because I was interested in Freud and there I was I hadn't even got to Freud and I was really excited with what I was doing.

We had to write on *The Plague*. So I bought five more copies of the book and gave them to my daughter and her husband and to three other friends and asked them to read it. Then we had them all around for dinner and discussed it. I even got some French wine! I taped the conversation. I had got some key themes I wanted to cover and then I just introduced them as we got into the meal. The tape recording was pretty awful, lots of clatter, but it was very good for what I wanted. I used these discussions in my essay. I haven't got the result yet. Even if I don't do very well, I gained an enormous amount out of it.

Most older retired students who enrol in award courses have undertaken study as a substantial and important component of their lives. They choose to study as something which is useful for them and which keeps them mentally active. They choose courses which project futures with valuable experiences and outcomes. However, courses come to an end and this prospect is not always one which older students view with a sense of pleasure. The question becomes, what to do next? Vera was over 70 years of age and was in her final semester of her degree.

I am going to miss my university study terribly. I have to be looking for something to do. I want to go overseas with my daughter next year. My husband would never travel, I think because of his health. He was frightened he would fall ill when he was away. Last year I went to China and to Europe. That was marvellous. I went to New Zealand, I loved that. We toured, but there were only six of us and everyone was most congenial and it was wonderful. It was really new for me. It was about three weeks I think. Then I went to Europe in September on about a fortnight's notice – with a Hungarian friend who was on her way to Budapest. We travelled with a Eurail ticket and worked our way east to Budapest gradually.

Vera was searching for a new future beyond her study. Presumably the travel would not be something which could sustain her entirely, if for no other reason, because of the expense. Mary was an elderly widow who had trodden a similar path to Vera, some years before. After she had completed her degree at the age of 68, she enrolled in a graduate degree and then at 70, enrolled in a Masters degree. She now runs a voluntary study group for students learning at a distance in her area and has become something of a mentor and advocate for 'younger' students (that is, those in their 30s and 40s who are just commencing study).

Losing a partner: finding study

Vera came to study after the death of her husband. This is something which seems common among older women, probably because they are more likely to survive their partners. Not only do they need to cope with absence of their partner, but also this removed restrictions associated with having to accommodate to a partner. This was more to do with the ways that the presence of a partner occupied a good part of their lives, rather than with any specific obstruction.

Vera started studying a few years before her husband's death.

I dropped out. I found it difficult to keep everything going. Then when my husband died, I thought I had to be very occupied so I picked up again. It has been quite hard at times, but it has been so important to me too.

Pat is another example of someone who chose to study after her bereavement.

He died, unfortunately, with cancer in 1979. I didn't want to rush anything after that period of time, but I knew I didn't want to stay in our previous home. I was being stifled, there was nothing down there at all. I went back and did English and all those sorts of things. I also had my music qualifications. Due to my brother-in-law's enthusiasm for study – he knew that I was very keen on study too – and I was always reading, he suggested I put it to some further use. So I investigated and I decided to approach the University, but I was really ill-advised at the time what subjects to do. They just said, well do an Arts degree. So I took up this Arts degree with the qualifications that I had and I undertook these subjects through distance education. It was during a history course that we went to do a quite close investigation of our local town. I became interested and I have always been interested in research and I did further investigations and I thought 'Well, I have got the best of two worlds here: research and study'.

Studying at a distance does not always have the degree of social interaction that the older person is seeking after their partner dies. Sometimes the 'traditional' part-time study is better, although this also places requirements and expectations which some older people prefer to avoid. Distance education does provide an important range of activities which occupy older people in a stimulating fashion and it is this which often provides the impetus and confidence for social encounters which occur outside of study, as with Vera's travels mentioned previously or with Mary's informal study groups.

Making contact

Some older people become involved in study with a friend which provides a source of mutual assistance as they help each other with their studies. Such students also find that tutorials, residential schools or weekend schools provide an encounter with a world of people – students and tutors – which can be very invigorating.

Mavis commenced study some years after her husband had died. She found herself in financial difficulties due to an inadequate pension and she had to sell the family home and move to a cheaper area so that she could have some money available to live on. She was an accomplished musician in her late 60s and she felt she had missed out on formal music qualifications during her life, principally due to the entrance requirements of schools of music which emphasized qualifications rather than performing ability.

I had a friendship that didn't develop and I was terribly upset about it. I thought I had better do something and study is what took its place.

The university had an information day so I thought I would go along and find out. I thought I would take the associate course, just for music. I was chatting to the tutor there and he said 'I would like you to take a BA degree'. I couldn't believe it. I came away like a dog with two tails!! I thought, 'He thinks I am worth that'. I think, basically I was in a way, but I hadn't got the confidence to really tackle it. I said I didn't think I would be able to afford it, and he said I would be able to get financial assistance. So that is how I started at the University, study at a distance.

I went to the residential school during the first year arts course. I enjoyed it and met a jolly nice crowd in the class. They had a concert one evening for students to perform in. I think there I was more interested in the concert than in learning because that is what I really want to do. One of the staff was a marvellous pianist and I had a lovely flame coloured dress that somebody had given me. So 'Madame' stood by the grand piano and sang Mozart's *Tell Me Fair Ladies* as though I had been doing it all my life. I had never sung so well and in this hall with all these students I thought I was really the cat's whiskers! And this is really what I should have done in my life, I mean it is too late now to reach the goal. Just before I came off the stage one of the young chaps, a student, he came up with a bouquet. The students in my class had rushed off to the nearest stall at the hospital and had a bouquet made up for me. I had never had a bouquet in my life before, well, that made my day. I went to friends after the residential school with my bouquet. I said 'I am taking these home with me, I know they are dropping, but I can't bear to part with them'. So I trundled all the way home with this nearly dead bouquet!

Mavis's experience with her class has an intensity and depth which was quite moving as she spoke about it. This is the sort of extremely positive learning experience that any student might undergo; however, for the older students, especially those who live alone after the death of a partner, the immersion into an active student group is an exciting contrast to their everyday lives. This potential is something of which both educators and learners need to be aware, because the responsibilities and consequences can have both positive and negative implications if these experiences are not understood and managed sensitively.

Such learning encounters, however, are not always pleasurable and positive. Occasionally, encounters with much younger and less experienced tutors can be agonizing for the older student. Gwynneth is in her late 50s and had retired to the country with her husband. She enrolled in a course to maintain her intellectual stimulation. She had always been a keen reader and had been involved in various community arts events during her life. After a very good experience with a tutor in her first year, she encountered some difficulties with her tutor in a subsequent course.

I was actually usually about a week and a half ahead of myself on this particular course. I wasn't on the science one last year, I was all the time running to catch up – it was a much harder course for me to do. Although my marks, strangely enough, haven't been as good on this one. But I think they mark differently, marking is totally different. Very pernickety is our tutor in this course. Ridiculous, actually in certain comments. I think she would put me off, if she had been my first tutor. I had a superb tutor last year. She really encouraged you. She made you feel as though you are getting somewhere and doing something, you know, it makes you want to go on. This one can deflate you if you don't watch it, she really can. She is very self-opinionated. She puts in some very interesting comments on the things that she does. She works hard on your assignments and comments, but some of them are so pernickety they make you spit.

One of my last assignments I had back – I loved doing it – we had to do a piece of imaginative writing and it is the first really imaginative piece that we had to do. I had a field day, I really enjoyed it. I was quite proud of what I had done in the end, and I said to everybody 'I will be proud of it now until I get the marks back, because I might not be so proud of it then'. When it came back I had 58 per cent which is the highest I have had from her. Last year I was getting 70s and 80s with sciences which is a hoot because science is difficult for me, but she seems to be quite stiff on marking. I passed but I still don't think of it as a good mark, I think it is fairly yukky really. I would still rather be in the 70s, I don't like being down at 58 – I don't consider that much cop. However, I have obviously got a lot to learn, so I will have to grin and bear it. I said something in my assignment about 'not everything that has been discovered in science has been for good'. Well, that implies that some things have been good, doesn't it? So she makes a little comment on the side 'Some things have been, surely?' and I thought 'What can I say then?' She really annoyed me, I thought about taking it up with her, but she is the same in a tutorial. She hasn't deflated me in a tutorial but she has some of the others, she can be very soul-destroying.

The other people I have asked, well they have had worse marks than me even, some of them, and one poor fellow on one thing she really did fail him, he got 25 per cent.

Gwynneth's experience is important because she believed that if she had had this tutor as her first she would probably have given up studying and stayed home, with her confidence shattered. However, the fact that she had worked hard at a difficult subject the first year and had an encouraging tutor meant that she was much more resilient when it came to a 'pernickety' tutor for a subsequent course in a subject area with which she had some considerable familiarity. Rather as Mavis felt like 'a dog with two tails' when a counsellor suggested she should enrol in a BA course, so it is with many older people who feel that by taking on a course they are venturing into something that they dearly want to do, but are very uncertain if they will be good enough. The younger students have their own uncertainties, of course, but they are much more likely to have completed secondary schooling and maybe have studied since leaving school; study experiences which are also very recent. For the older student it can be much more daunting, and appropriate support from tutors is very important, not just to their success as students, but also for their self-concepts and quality of life. Clearly, educational organizations need to select, prepare and monitor their tutors carefully, especially in the initial stages of their employment.

Ideological differences between younger staff and older students can be a source of strain, as the following example from Amy shows. Amy had led a tough life after her husband died young and left her with two young children. She took over her husband's fairground amusement arcade business which she ran for nearly 25 years. She had made her way in the male-dominated world of the travelling fairgrounds and, having retired at 70 years of age, decided to enrol in distance education course to broaden her mind.

I did the social science course which I didn't really enjoy. It was fine as long as you remain detached from it because the place is absolutely heaving with banner-carrying fanatics when you do the social science course. They are either extreme right, extreme left, extreme feminists, extreme the opposite or whatever, you know! Life is very hard for us older ones in the middle who've seen a bit of life who try and laugh now and again. There was a delightful young man (Nick)[1] on that course and there were a couple of girls in our group who were raving feminists and Nick would only have to say one sentence and the tutorial would be destroyed. Because the woman tutor just used to let them get away with it and Nick would just sit there, chewing his pen. I had a go at them after the tutorial. I said, 'His wife is a qualified teacher who is at home because she has two young children and because she wants to be. Nick worships the ground she walks on and she worships the ground he walks on and they are perfectly happy and know far more about relationships than you two seem to'. They said, 'Well you have been on your own'. I replied, 'Yes, through no choice. I certainly don't recommend being on your own as a way to bring up children, and don't quarrel with me because I know, I have done it'.

Amy was a strong enough character to be able to stand up for her views and not to be intimidated by tutors or students she felt were pushing their own ideologies. She was even protective of Nick whom she felt was in danger of giving up his course because of his experiences in the tutorials. Amy believed that her generation went through the War to defeat the fascists and preserve democracy; she also had lived a tough life since. Hence, she was not too enamoured which what she saw as extremist ideologies masquerading as social science. Older students are perhaps a little more sceptical than younger students of current ideological fashions. Whether it is a social science course, or one which is dealing with health and budgeting, there is less likely to be enthusiastic acceptance, unless it harmonizes with their experience and common-sense understanding of the topic.

Learning styles and approaches for older students

Older students typically have different study circumstances and learning approaches to younger students. Partly this is due to the lifestyle offered by retirement as against the working parent, for example, who is trying to squeeze study into a busy day. It is also due to changes in memory and concentration abilities.

David, in his late 50s, reflected on his previous abilities.

> I think it is easier to retain knowledge when you are younger. People talk a lot about the extra things you put into study when you are of mature years (as they so nicely put it), and you do – life experience and all that sort of thing. On the other hand, I don't think that your memory is nearly as good as in your 40s, or in your 40s as it was even in your 30s. I don't think mine is, but that might be just me.

Older students often believe that they spend more time studying than their younger counterparts. Sometimes this is due to interest, as Amy explains.

> I spend a lot more time studying than most people, a lot more. I am not sure whether it is well-directed study. I find it interesting. At the end of the units, knowing that people haven't got time to breathe, they put lists of further reading which I find fascinating. If you want a good pass you don't have to do it. You have to stick with what they say in the unit.

Vera found that it was more of a necessity for her to spend a lot of extra time on her studies, but she was not sure that it was time that was rewarded.

I find it a struggle I might say. Essays I find I spend far too much time on them and the longer I spend the worse they are – I don't get High Distinctions all the time! I often flounder because it is very hard. You think you are flexible, but it is very hard to think along a completely new line when you're older. You have been brought up in a culture and educated in a school in one line of thought, you know. To make a different approach and also to find out things, research them yourself, they were all new to me until a later age. You are bound by your early culture, however much you think you are not. You are a rebel when you are young and that is silly too. I was a bit of a rebel, but it is very difficult when you are much older, some can do it, and some perhaps are able to get outside that. I try.

Vera explains how the positive aspects of an older person's circumstances can be balanced against the negative aspects of deteriorating learning capacities.

Something with an older person – other older people will tell you – I find in the afternoon at home I can read and take notes, but I tend to fall asleep and I have sometimes found my notes in a squiggle. However, if I go to the library – which I am free to do of course – it never happens at the library, so that is why I would rather work out there. Maybe it is the person talking in the next carrel. I spend a couple of hours. I would spend all day if I could, but I have got a lot of other interests and I try and make family and friends the first two priorities because they are important and study is third priority. You swap things around if an assignment is due, study might be first priority for a while.

The more self-paced nature of open and distance education courses suits older students particularly well. They can fit their studies into the lifestyle that they wish to maintain for themselves and balancing their priorities is generally easier than for the younger student. However, this self-paced nature is lost when a residential school comes around. Residential schools are usually filled to the brim with activities which even the youngest and fittest find exhausting. For the older students, their needs and capacities have been overlooked as they struggle to study all day and disco all night! Mavis is a person who likes parties and social activities, but she found residential schools too demanding.

I suppose a lot of it at my age was speed. You have got to be quite honest, haven't you. I mean I have got a quick brain but to absorb things at the speed of the residential school was immensely difficult. I found it was the speed and then you had to absorb so much. It was really heavy going. It was about 12 hours a day by the time you were finished with lectures and what have you. At lunchtime I used to go up to my room and relax, so that I had enough steam for the afternoon session.

Everything goes very fast. You have to move from one place to another and also trying to find out where it was. I had a lot of walking about to the next class. I am pretty fit, but I know of some older people who couldn't take it and would have a sleep in the afternoon. Of course, after you have raced around all day and had lectures through to the evening, then there's the disco. You feel you ought to get involved, there's tutors there too. And I like a good dance, I do! But I need a couple of weeks to recover – honestly, I really do.

The use of face-to face sessions in open and distance education has very many important features for all students and, as has been shown previously, there are often some powerful benefits in such contact. However, the more self-paced nature of open and distance education is lost in these circumstances and, clearly, there can be significant learning (and health) problems if older (and even younger) students are pushed too hard. It seems that more self-pacing could be of benefit in such face-to-face encounters as residential schools and weekend schools.

Some older students find that their learning is supported by the younger members of their families, which often helps them sustain their confidence and commitment to their studies. Amy lives with her daughter and son-in-law and her grandchildren.

Oh, my family certainly don't get in the way of my study. They are a pain the neck! When I say I don't want to bother studying any more, they keep saying 'Yes you are, come on, everybody out of granny's room'. When there is an assignment due back in the post you know, my grandson comes in with the envelope 'It's for you granny, from the university'. I say 'I don't want to know!'. They like to read what the tutor has to say about me. They fall about laughing in the kitchen over breakfast. I get things like 'Very well written' – they are always very kind about my English you see – 'and you put down the points in very good order.' Then the family choruses, 'BUT!' And then the tutor points to some matter of detail that I have omitted.

Amy's circumstances, given her good humour, are ones which support her studying. The family provides her with encouragement when needed and the privacy to study when necessary. Now in her 70s, she finds that the comfort and support of family life and the independence of study are providing her with a fulfilling retirement.

Lifelong learning: literally

The older students' stories which have been told in this chapter provide a glimpse of the ways some older people use study as an important *raison d'être*. The intrinsic merits of study are often uppermost, even though, for some courses, there are also significant extrinsic merits to do with being able to manage one's life better. It seems that study is often undertaken within the first few years (if not months) of retirement, which means that, eventually, there is a problem of what to do when each course finishes. Some older people have a seemingly continuous flow of short, non-award courses, such as those offered by various adult education groups, local authorities and bodies such as U3A. Others opt for much longer award courses, such as degree courses, which often mean six to ten years of part-time independent study at a distance. As the end of these long periods approaches, the dependency on study becomes evident. Vera makes the point.

It is much harder than I thought it would be, studying for a degree. But that is because of me I think. It is so stimulating, it is not boring. Unless I can do something else when I finish, I will miss it. Perhaps I ought to do home maintenance or something more practical, perhaps that will be just as good. I must do something, that's for sure.

Pat provides a poignant statement which aptly encapsulates the theme of learning through life, which has been a thread throughout this and previous chapters.

As long as I live I will always be learning. The day I stop learning they will put me six feet under!

Note

1 He was actually 44 years of age! By chance I interviewed him as part of
   my research and he said very little about this event.

Chapter 9

Endframes: uncovering the diversities of learners' contexts

As a young school teacher in the early 1970s, I tried to understand my students fairly well. I lived in the same community and I knew some of their parents. I understood what they saw on television, what teams they supported, what games they played, what music they liked. They seemed to be fairly uncomplicated individuals. They had their differences, of course, but they shared so many things in common, including a limited experience of life, that I thought I could teach them pretty well. I was also studying at university part-time for my Masters degree, which gave me a certain empathy with them as we all tried to fit our 'homework' around our pleasures in life.

One day in 1974 I had two new students in one of my classes, they had arrived from Chile and spoke limited English. They sat quietly in class and were model students in every respect except their work, which was poor in comparison with their peers. Their quiet disquieted me. Who were these children? What were they like? How could I get to know them? My enquiries of others and conversations with them over the ensuing weeks helped me to know them, but I realized that the more I knew about them, and the more I knew of the experiences they had undergone, the less I really knew about them. They were refugees from the bloody coup which had overthrown Allende. Their experiences and previous home circumstances were very different from my own and that of my other students. As they were from soccer-saturated South America, I tried to discuss this game and bring some of my other students into the discussion who were from families who also came from soccer-saturated nations. This worked, up to a point, a point at which I realized that soccer and soccer grounds signified different things to us. In my childhood, a soccer ground meant going with my father to see Guildford City play, or later to go to Highbury to see the Gunners blaze. For my Chilean students, Santiago soccer stadium meant the place where their fathers (or other relatives) met incarceration, torture and blazing guns. As a young teacher I wasn't sure how to teach people I didn't really understand. My teacher education had encouraged and prepared me to teach in ways which related to students, but *who* were *these* students?[1]

Now I am working in distance education where we plan courses three years before they are offered and usually run them for three to five years before a revised or 'remade' version replaces it. Questions that trouble me in distance education are: Who are 'my' students? What will they make of my course? What will they make of it in a few years time? For distance educators, in particular, there is a student void which needs to be filled in order for them to teach. It seems that distance educators fill up this student void with what they imagine their students will be like. But, as this is based substantially on their previous experience, it is difficult to imagine students whom one does not yet know and whose experiences one does not share. This is a major problem when distance educators from the 'developed' world work on creating or updating courses for 'developing' world contexts.[2] The task is easier for the teacher or trainer working in a setting where they have closer contact with the people who will eventually study their courses. Indeed, the curriculum of those courses may well be negotiated or framed in consultation with them. As was mentioned in Chapter 1, such circumstances are pedagogical leaps of faith rather than bungee jumps into an educational abyss, which is more like the distance educator's lot.

Whether working in a classroom, training department, open learning centre, or distance education institution, the question remains for the good teacher or trainer: who are my students? Of course, a teacher or trainer who poses such a question is moving beyond the 'empty vessel' or 'banking' models of education.[3] They are seeing adult learners as people with histories and contexts which will affect the ways they learn in relation to the way they are taught.[4] The dynamic nature of the teaching-learning process means that when a teacher reaches a good understanding of the learner, their teaching changes and, thus, the learning and the learner also change. The previous chapters demonstrate that it is practically impossible to understand *the learner* at all. Rather it is a case of understanding *learners* as a diverse, heterogeneous and changing body of people.

The preceding chapters have addressed issues which stem directly from the concerns and contexts of a variety of students, be they to do with gender, age, work, money or whatever. The students' experiences, views and circumstances which have been presented reveal the sort of problem I had as a school teacher with my Chilean students. The more one knows of the diversity of students' experiences, views and circumstances, the more uncertain one becomes as a teacher or trainer. Previous homogeneous conceptions of *the student* are exploded into a galaxy of individual, unique students. The more one finds out, the more one realizes there remains to find out. It is rather like settling down to sleep under the stars in the Australian desert on a moonless night. As one's eyes become more accustomed to the dark, the stars between the stars between the stars become clear. If it wasn't for falling asleep, it appears more stars would be revealed for ever.

However, human cultures have ways of framing human experiences – of stars and students! – so that they can be understood and explained. This book has framed students' experiences into a series of chapters which address themes which the practitioner can use both to understand and to address the issues. On occasions, the overlaps between these frames have been made clear, but often each chapter has tended to focus on its particular themes to the exclusion of the other issues. So, for example, the chapter on gender considered issues that were pertinent to that theme, but issues to do with age, power or money, for instance, are also gendered. The interconnections are very important for understanding students holistically – that is, to see (and teach) students as complete and complex entities whose wholeness is more than the sum of their particular characteristics.[5] It should also be stated that there were other issues which could have been explored and that the ones covered in this book simply represent the ones that seem to be most pertinent.

The shape of the book and the ways the issues and students' stories are selected, represented and discussed, stem from the author's experiences and interests. However, there are, of course, the readers' own experiences which both help to frame their personal understandings of the learners' issues in this book, and also help to add to their stock of knowledge of learners' experiences in general. Some of the students' stories in this book will probably harmonize with individual reader's own 'insider' experiences as students, teachers or trainers. Other stories will probably be viewed more as if the reader were an 'outsider'. For the open and distance educator, generally, most of the learners present themselves as 'outsiders' at the outset and the best teachers usually try to bring their students 'inside' their courses using a variety of strategies based on their own personal experiences and predilections.[6] I shall pursue these matters further, starting with the way personal and local knowledge informs our practice and moving to the ways broader, theoretical frames can aid our understanding of students.

Open and distance educators have several ways to fill the student voids which frame their own course development and teaching. They use their 'common-sense' knowledge of previous students, of friends and family who are or who have been students and, perhaps most importantly and most often forgotten, of *themselves* when they were students. These sorts of personal knowledge of being a learner are very important in the teaching process for those who have to teach at a distance. Distance educators project into the student void an array of knowledge of the student experiences which enables them to prejudge the learning encounters which will occur sometime in the future. In effect, every teacher or trainer does this when they plan their classes; however, face-to-face teachers also have actual experiences of their students – or good 'intelligence' in the way that Liz Curie exemplifies in Chapter 1 – which they can use in their planning, and they have the interactive capacity in the classroom to vary their teaching in response to the students' needs.

Given that personal experience and knowledge of learners forms an important part of the open and distance educators' resources, it seems important for the good teacher or trainer to do two things. One is to recognize explicitly that their experience and knowledge is important to their work, whether or not this has been visible or invisible in the past. The other is to reflect critically on that knowledge and experience by setting it against the sorts of diversity of students' experiences we have seen in previous chapters.[7] Thus, by comparing one's own experiences and knowledge of learners with those of someone whose actual learning experience is quite different, then the taken-for-granted assumptions about what counts as good teaching for all students, based on the the assumed 'known' student, are called into question. Don Markovitz, in Chapter 1, called some of his experiences into question in this way. The students' stories in this book have shown that, for instance, while some students study because it fits with their work and they receive paid leave and financial support from their employers for doing so, others are studying for entirely personal reasons, in their own time and entirely at their own expense.

It is deceptively easy to develop courses on the basis of taken-for-granted assumptions about students' circumstances, such as their access to libraries or study centres, spare time to study, reading and writing abilities, interests in the subject, physical abilities, etc. However, the previous chapters show that, for such assumptions, there are many possible variations, some of which will render the assumptions incorrect and counterproductive for a number of students' learning. For example, some students find that their work and family commitments make it very difficult to obtain sufficient 'quality time' for their studies; others have mobility or transport difficulties which effectively prevent their access to libraries or study centres. Courses which are planned on the assumption that all students will have sufficient 'quality time' and access to libraries and study centres, are *designed to fail*, or rather they are *designed to fail* some of *their students*. Such design and development faults should be anathema to good teachers, but especially to open educators who (should) have as one of their goals openness to the needs and contexts of their students. The problem is that if such educators work on the uncritical use of their personal knowledge and experience, they risk designing to fail.

Apart from reflecting critically on one's knowledge and experiences of learners, there are also deliberate ways that educators and their institutions can go about understanding the diversity of learners' experiences and contexts. Typically, institutional surveys are used to evaluate courses or educational services. Sometimes, forms of 'market' surveys are used prior to course approval or accreditation to ascertain the need for a proposed course, but often these are sent to experts in the field, employers or professional bodies rather than to prospective students. It is often difficult for educational institutions to survey prospective students for exactly the reason raised in Chapter 1. That is, especially in open and distance education where long lead-times are the rule, the 'prospective' students do not even know of the possibility of the course at that stage, so how can an institution identify and survey such people? Of course, it is possible, especially on courses which are likely to appeal to a defined clientele, such as an occupational group or a group with an existing educational need (for example, a job skills course or an English as a second language course), to send a survey to people who are likely to be prospective students.

It is also the case that some forms of market survey are, at least partly, about creating a prospective market. So an institution which surveys prospective students may actually be beginning the process of constructing those people into future students. The blanket survey, which is distributed generally but which requires people to return their responses and has the option of including their name and address 'so that we can keep you informed about this new exciting development', is providing the institution with a database for its first pre-enrolment mailing. For people working in industrial settings, the 'market' survey is typically aimed at specific groups in the workplace and also has the effect of creating a perceived need or demand for the intended course. This is not to suggest that, in both the industrial and institutional contexts, such surveys represent a self-serving attempt on the part of the educators to create a course and, therefore, work and income for themselves. Rather, educational entrepreneurialism requires not only good judgements about community and industrial needs for education and training, but also good implementation processes, which include forms of 'marketing'.

One important potential of the approaches which open and distance educators make to prospective students through surveys, meetings with prospective students, etc., is the capacity to understand more of the experiences and contexts of those prospective students. It seems that there is often a concern for making the curriculum relevant and shaping the assessment to fit, for example, people's work or professional contexts. However, there is a capacity to begin the process of ascertaining something of the diversity of the student clientele. The preceding chapters in this book have opened up the key areas which could be pursued. For example, issues to do with age, gender and family relationships, money, social and educational backgrounds could be investigated. Using this information – and there is no point in collecting the information unless it is used[8] – can have a significant impact on the teaching and learner support strategies employed on a course. This seems to be especially important for open educators because their proclaimed intention to be 'open' implies that they need to understand what counts as openness in the experience of the learners. In order to be open to a diversity of students requires understanding, from the outset, what this diversity means for their practices as open educators. In this book, the significance of the diversity of learners' experiences and contexts has been revealed and the open and distance educator can use this knowledge to frame their planning and course development phases, including the use of strategies to find out *who* are their prospective students.

One of the matters which has unfolded in the course of this book is the way in which learners change and develop as they engage with their courses. This is particularly the case for those on fairly lengthy part-time degree programmes which span several years, but there is evidence of smaller changes, too, for those on courses of shorter duration.[9] We have seen that some of these changes affect the students deeply such that their personal and family relationships are permanently altered. Other changes are more directly related to the learning which takes place on the courses and the ways in which the students adapt to their new knowledge and skills.

Therefore, understanding the diversity of students is not simply a case of, for example, surveying or interviewing students as they enrol, or of being a first year tutor receptive to the broader nature of students' contexts. The former is merely a cross-section at a given point in time and the tutor's receptivity is a mere thread of encounters with (usually) a fragment of the student community. It is analogous to attempting to understand global weather processes using an array of readings at one point in time or, in the tutor's case, from a set of readings over a period of time from one weather station. The global weather system is a dynamic system which has certain repetitive general patterns (seasons, for example) and it is very difficult to understand and predict. Adult learners *en masse* are every bit as difficult to understand and predict and yet we need to do so with a reasonable degree of certainty to be good educators. At the local level, this means ensuring that we actually do sufficient regular research to maintain reliable 'recordings' and accurate 'forecasts'.[10] More broadly, it means having practice and research-based understandings (theories) about adult open and distance education learners' experiences and contexts.[11]

So here lies the challenge for open and distance educators. Adult students *en masse* are as dynamic and chaotic as the global weather system. The preceding chapters have featured some of the major issues which stem from students' accounts of the diversity of their learning experiences and contexts. In this chapter it has been argued that, in order to be good open and distance educators, understanding students' experiences and contexts needs to be a process which is sustained from the course development and pre-enrolment phases, through the learning phases, to course completion. The challenge is to develop and maintain approaches which enable students to have their voices heard and for the open and distance educators and their institutions to be able to listen and understand the practical implications of what is being said. Learners should also recognize that they are part of a diverse body of people whose interests need to be voiced, and whose stories need to be told.

Notes

1   I have previously used this account and some of the questions it raises in Evans, T D (1991) 'Knowing the voids: understanding the distance student in a postmodern world', in Tait, A (ed.) *The Student, Community and Curriculum*: *Proceedings of the International Perspectives on Open and Distance Education conference*, University of Cambridge, September.

2 Several commentators have elaborated on this point. See, for example, Ansu-Kyeremeh, K (1991) 'Distance education in a developing context: Ghana' in Evans, T D and King, B (eds) *Beyond the Text: Contemporary writing on distance education*, Geelong: Deakin University Press, pp. 137–51; Arger, G (1985) 'Promise and reality: a critical analysis of literature on distance education in the Third World', *Journal of Distance Education*, 2, 1, 41–58; Guy, R (1991) 'Distance education and the developing world', in Evans, T D and King, B (eds) *Beyond the text: Contemporary writing on distance education*, Geelong: Deakin University Press, pp. 152–75; Guy, R (1992) 'Distance education in Papua New Guinea: reflections on reality', *Open Learning*, 7, 1, 28–39.

3 Paulo Freire used the notion of 'banking education' to typify what is a dominant form of education in modernist societies. From this viewpoint knowledge (cash) is deposited in the minds (accounts) of people for them to use productively (derive interest). See Freire, P (1972) *Pedagogy of the Oppressed*, Harmondsworth: Penguin. Helen Modra has discussed this and other of Freire's ideas in relation to her work in distance education. See, Modra, H (1989) 'Using journals to encourage critical thinking at a distance', in Evans, T D and Nation, D E (eds) *Critical Reflections on Distance Education*, London: Falmer Press, pp. 123–46. Instructional design can be criticized for reflecting a 'banking' model of education. It is concerned with framing the educational process in terms of the knowledge to be deposited, hence a good deal of 'investment planning' takes place in the form of concept mapping and the like. However, for the approach to education I am adopting in this book, and in my teaching, I believe it is important to see learners as human agents in the (their) educational processes who will, whether we like it or not, actively construct their learning in their interests. Daryl Nation and I have discussed this and related matters in some detail. See Evans, T D and Nation, D E (1989) 'Critical reflections in distance education', in Evans T D and Nation D E (eds) *Critical Reflections on Distance Education*, London: Falmer Press, pp. 237–52; Evans, T D and Nation, D E (1989) 'Dialogue in practice, research and theory in distance education', *Open Learning*, 4, 2, 37–43; Evans, T D and Nation, D E (1992) 'Theorising open and distance education', *Open Learning*, 7, 2, 3–13 (republished in Tait, A (ed.) (1993) *Key Issues in Open Learning*, London: Longman, pp. 45–62).

4 There are several writers who have addressed approaches to educating adults which see the process as requiring not only receptivity to the learners' contexts, but also a recognition of the dynamic (and, for some,

empowering) nature of the teaching-learning process. As one might expect, there are also differences between the approaches espoused by these authors; however, a selection from some of the key figures would include the following: Boud, D and Griffin, V (eds) (1987) *Appreciating Adults Learning*, London: Kogan Page; Boud, D, Keogh, R and Walker, D (eds) (1985) *Reflection: Turning experience into learning*, London: Kogan Page; Brookfield, S (1986) *Understanding and Facilitating Adult Learning*, San Francisco: Jossey Bass; Brookfield, S (1987) *Developing Critical Thinkers: Challenging adults to explore alternative ways of thinking and acting*, San Francisco: Jossey Bass; Knowles, M (1978) *The Adult Learner: A neglected species*, Houston: Gulf Publishing; Knowles, M (1980) *The Modern Practice of Adult Education*, Chicago: Association Press; Mezirow, J (1991) *Transformative Dimensions of Adult Learning*, San Francisco: Jossey Bass; Mezirow, J and associates (1990) *Fostering Critical Reflection in Adulthood: A guide to transformative and emancipatory learning*, San Francisco: Jossey Bass.

Liz Burge and Margaret Haughey, both separately and jointly, have brought adult learning theories to bear on distance education. See, for example, Burge, L (1988) 'Beyond andragogy: some explorations for distance learning design', *Journal of Distance Education*, 3, 1, 5–23; Burge, L and Haughey, M (1993) 'Transformative learning in reflective practice', in Evans, T D and Nation, D E (eds) *Reforming Open and Distance Education*, London: Kogan Page, pp. 88–112; Haughey, M (1991) 'Confronting the pedagogical issues', *Open Learning*, 6, 3, 14–23.

5   There has been a growing body of research and writing which has adopted holistic approaches to understanding students and their learning. For a selection of approaches see, Marton, F, Hounsell, D and Entwistle, N (1984) *The Experience of Learning*, Edinburgh: Scottish Academic Press. For work which is particularly related to theory and research in open and distance education see, Grace, M (1990) 'Hermeneutic theory in research in distance education', in Evans, T D (ed.) *Research in Distance Education 1*, Geelong: Deakin University, pp. 21–35; Morgan, A R (1992) 'Theorising adult change and development through research in distance education', in Evans, T D and Juler, P E (eds) *Research in Distance Education 2*, Geelong: Deakin University Press, pp. 81–8, see especially pp. 83–4; Morgan, A R, Taylor E and Gibbs, G (1982) 'Understanding the distance learner as a whole person', in Daniel, J *et al.* (eds) *Learning at a Distance: A world perspective*, Edmonton: Athabasca University/International Council for Distance Education, pp. 83–113.

6   Daryl Nation is an interesting practitioner in this regard. He uses personal reflections as a teaching strategy, not only to teach the conceptual material of the course, but also to engender a personal engagement by students and himself with the course. See, Nation, D E (1987) 'Some reflections upon teaching sociology at a distance', *Distance Education*, 8, 2, 190–207; 'Teaching texts and independent learning', in Evans, T D and King, B (eds) *Beyond the Text: Contemporary writing on distance education*, Geelong: Deakin University Press, pp. 101–129.

7   The case for critical reflection in distance education has been argued elsewhere. See, Evans, T D and Nation, D E (eds) (1989) *Critical Reflections on Distance Education*, London: Falmer Press, Chapters 2 and 12; several examples can be found in that book and in Evans, T D and Nation, D E (eds) (1993) *Reforming Open and Distance Education*, London: Kogan Page; Evans, T D (1991) 'An epistemological orientation to critical reflection in distance education', in Evans, T D and King, B (eds) *Beyond the Text: Contemporary writing on distance education*, Geelong: Deakin University Press, pp. 7–18.

8   Alistair Morgan has railed against 'mindless data collection' by educational institutions whose surveys seem to do little more than fill computer discs or questionnaire storage boxes. He has argued that there is a strong case for reforming such applied research and grounding it in theory, and also using this to understand adult change and development. See, Morgan, A R (1990) 'Whatever happened to the silent scientific revolution? Research, theory and practice in distance education', in Evans, T D (ed.) *Research in Distance Education 1*, Geelong: Deakin University Press, pp. 9–20; Morgan, A R (1992) 'Theorising adult change and development through research in distance education', in Evans, T D and Juler, P A (eds) *Research in Distance Education 2*, Geelong: Deakin University Press, pp. 81–8.

9   Nick Farnes has charted the life and educational changes of continuing education students and shown how these changes can be related to each other, both graphically and conceptually. See, Farnes, N (1992) 'Life course analysis in distance education', in Evans, T D and Juler, P A (eds) *Research in Distance Education 2*, Geelong: Deakin University Press, pp. 89–104. He points to the need for both more research and theorizing in this area of adult change and development. In terms of the argument in this chapter, it can be seen that the scope for such research is broad and can be embedded in the planning and development phases of open and distance education courses as well as in the form of

longitudinal research throughout students' courses.

10 Gleick has told the story of Chaos Theory, including one of its most influential metaphors, the 'butterfly effect', whereby it is argued that the dynamic complexity of weather systems is such that the movement of a butterfly's wings may produce effects on the system which lead eventually to a storm elsewhere; Gleick, J (1987) *Chaos: The making of a new science*, London: Sphere Books. So, by using the weather system as a metaphor for the education of adults, it may need to be recognized that one student 'stretching their wings' may lead eventually to an 'educational storm'! Chris Bigum has applied some of the ideas of Chaos Theory to distance education; Bigum, C (1990) 'Chaos and educational computing: deconstructing distance education', in Evans, T D (ed.) *Research in Distance Education 1*, Geelong: Deakin University Press, pp. 72–82.

11 This raises not just theoretical and research problems for distance education, but also problems for distance education processes and practices themselves. The research problems are ones concerned with the 'absences' in our work: absences of omission in the sense that, say, Minnis and Morgan outline, and absences of knowing uncovered or suggested by research itself; Minnis, J R (1985) 'Ethnography, case study, grounded theory and distance education research', *Distance Education*, 6, 2, 189–98; Morgan, A R (1984) 'A report on qualitative methodologies in research in distance education', *Distance Education*, 5, 2, 252–67; Morgan, A R (1990) 'Whatever happened to the silent revolution? Research, theory and practice in distance education', in Evans, T D (ed.) *Research in Distance Education 1*, Geelong: Deakin University Press, pp. 9–20.

The problems of open and distance education processes and practices are created by the uncertainties that we now face about the knowns, the givens, the taken-for-granteds in our work. If it can be seen that there are considerable voids in educators' understandings of the people they plan to teach, then what does this say about the educational planning and development undertaken on the students' behalf? Cziko has argued, using postmodernist science, that educational research – of the positivist empiricist kind – is fatally flawed and cannot predict or control the educational outcomes that it purports to do; Cziko, G A (1989) 'Unpredictability and indeterminism in human behavior: arguments and implications for educational research', *Educational Researcher*, April, 17–25. Such arguments shatter the foundations of instructional design – except, perhaps, in the most tightly controlled and narrow training settings. But the broader implications of the argument are that qualitative research leads towards not only a better understanding of students – as Cziko argues – but also to an appreciation of the voids in our knowledge of those students.

Margaret Grace has discussed some related problems stemming from her work with hermeneutic theory; see Grace, M (1990) 'Hermeneutic theory in research in distance education', in Evans, T D (ed.) *Research in Distance Education 1*, Geelong: Deakin University Press, pp. 21–35; Grace, M (1992) 'Communication and meaning: the first year experience of off-campus study', PhD thesis, Geelong: Deakin University. Patti Lather's work on postmodernist feminist research and theorizing is very stimulating and provides an entrée which critical open and distance educators will find fruitful; see, Lather, P (1991) *Getting Smart: Feminist research and pedagogy within the postmodern*, London: Routledge.